TRAVELS ON THE BREAD LINE

'AN ENTERTAINING AND INSPIRING ACCOUNT, FULL OF COURAGE AND COMEDY'
Katie Fforde

FRAN ADAMS

TRAVELS ON THE BREAD LINE

'AN ENTERTAINING AND INSPIRING ACCOUNT, FULL OF COURAGE AND COMEDY'
Katie Fforde

MEMOIRS

Cirencester

Published by Memoirs

MEMOIRS
PUBLISHING

25 Market Place, Cirencester, Gloucestershire, GL7 2NX
info@memoirsbooks.co.uk www.memoirspublishing.com

First published in England, March 2013

Book jacket design Ray Lipscombe

ISBN 978-1-909544-34-5

Printed in England

CONTENTS

～

INTRODUCTION

My desire to embark on a cycling holiday in a foreign country began as a fleeting fancy, but as each year passed without us being able to afford any holiday at all, it grew into a passion which could not be repressed. I just wanted to jump on my bike and cycle off into the unknown. The trouble was, I wasn't brave enough to go alone. I would need my teenage sons, Pete and Malc, for company.

Finally, in 1987, by wangling it so that nearly all the boys' Christmas and birthday presents were of a camping or cycling nature, we acquired all that was necessary for a basic holiday. Nothing would stop me now, although I was warned that my old bike might break up if I hit a pothole.

In August of that year the great day arrived. Having overcome some last-minute qualms, I finally set off with Pete, Malc and their friend Tom for what would prove to us to be the holiday of a lifetime, even though it was only across the English channel to Brittany. We were beset with difficulties from the word go, but in spite of this we had the time of our lives.

But that was not the end of the story. Our 'holiday of a lifetime' only served to fuel my passion to do it all over again.

So from the moment we arrived home I began secretly to scrimp and save, hoping we might one day repeat that sunny, fun-filled holiday.

There were times when it seemed highly unlikely that it would ever happen, but at last my selfish dreams were realised and we set off once more for sunny Brittany. Tom was not with us this time, but we didn't think it would make much difference.

However this holiday proved to be nothing like we'd expected. In fact it wasn't really like a holiday at all. By the end of it Pete and Malc had stopped being rival siblings and become friends, while I had discovered what I really wanted in life.

To Malissa

With Best Wishes

from Fran X

To my sons Pete and Malc, for coming with me

ACKNOWLEDGEMENTS

I would like to thank Dervla Murphy, who inspired me in the first place, and to give special thanks to Katie Fforde, for typing out my transcribed diary notes while in exchange I did her housework.

My thanks also to Elizabeth Snow, Cherry Ann Knott, Trish Mills and Jill and Malcolm Pritchard for their editing. Also to Sheila Morrison, Sue Gibbs and Sue Breens for their constructive suggestions.

Finally I would like to thank my next-door neighbour, Sylvia Harrington, for giving me the bright red cloth from which I made our very visible tent-roll covers.

PART ONE

SUMMER 1987

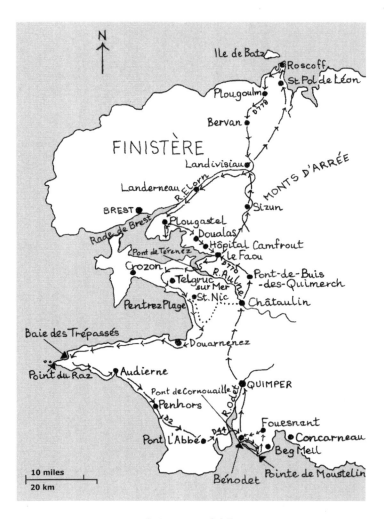

Brittany 1987

CHAPTER ONE

Departure

Stroud, Wednesday August 19 1987

It was 5.30 am when I looked at the clock. With so much on my mind, there was no point in lying in bed any longer. Creeping out quietly, so as not to wake my husband Jim, I tiptoed down the two flights of stairs to our basement kitchen and made a large tin of gingerbread. We would take some with us and leave the rest for him. I'd already done loads of baking the day before, so for a few days at least he'd be left with something nice to eat. That eased my conscience a bit.

I was taking our two sons, Pete and Malc, aged 15 and 13, on a cycling holiday in France, and leaving Jim behind. I wasn't feeling at all excited, though I should have been. This holiday had been a long time coming. Living on the breadline as we were, I had been scrimping and saving for ages to get everything we needed.

Some years earlier I had read a book by Dervla Murphy called *Full Tilt*, which told how she had cycled all the way from Ireland to India. A seed had been sown in my mind. As each year passed without us ever affording any holidays at all, apart from the odd day trip to Weston-super-Mare, it had grown into a passion which spurred me into action. I was nearly 43 and nothing was going to stop me now.

I craved for adventure; to cycle off into the unknown. However, not being as brave as Dervla, I would need my boys for company. Our 'unknown' would be humble Brittany. Of course it was only across the Channel, but as we'd never been abroad before, it *felt* like an adventure. We'd heard that it was sparsely populated, with lots of quiet roads to cycle on.

Having used the excuse that my teenage sons needed to practise their French, I'd managed to wangle it so that most of their birthday and Christmas presents were related to cycling or camping. Eventually we had all the equipment we needed. If we didn't go this year it could be too late. Next year Pete would be taking his French GCSE and by then he'd have turned sixteen, so I'd have to pay adult fares for him.

Pete had asked if his friend Tom could come with us and I'd said yes, especially as I felt rather sorry for him. His parents had split up and he'd recently acquired a stepmum, plus two young step-siblings. I thought a holiday would do him good.

I'd expected the rail fare to set me back quite a bit, so I was nicely surprised that it didn't. With a Family Railcard for £15, we could get from Stroud to Plymouth return for just £20 for myself and £1 each for the three boys (as long as we didn't travel on a Friday or Saturday). I thought that was pretty good.

Spaces for bikes on the train from Cheltenham to Plymouth had to be booked beforehand at an extra cost of £3 each. Unfortunately we couldn't reserve bike spaces on the Stroud to Cheltenham train, as this wasn't an Inter-City one.

But the man in Stroud ticket office told us not to worry; there wouldn't be a problem.

The ferry fares were staggering. From fourteen years of age you were considered an adult. It was age sixteen on the trains and seventeen on National coaches. I was aghast to learn that three of us would each have to pay £56, considering that our family of four managed on less than £100 a week.

We consulted a well-travelled cyclist who lived up our lane, and on his advice bought two adult tickets and two child ones. Now my biggest problem was going to be how to get my six-foot son past the ferry officials. Still, I could worry about that later.

Pete had grown so much in the last couple of years and become quite mature. If anything he was a bit serious. I felt he might feel responsible for us on holiday. He could mend lots of things on a bike and was full of innovative ideas. His French wasn't bad, either.

My boys were not alike in looks or nature. Pete was tall and dark haired, whereas Malc was broader with fair hair. He was forever acting the clown. Sometimes he and I would only have to look at one another for a few seconds before we'd burst out laughing, even if he wasn't making a funny face. Like his mum though, he was a bit of a worrier. Pete tended to keep his worries hidden.

Tom was tall like Pete, but thinner, with reddish hair and freckles. All I knew about him was that he was as fit and enthusiastic as my two and full of light-hearted wit, but prone to asthma and eczema.

We'd had lots of last-minute setbacks. For instance, I'd decided to paint my bike frame with Hammerite paint because it was so tatty. When I'd taken the rusty carrier off the back, it had disintegrated at the boltholes. So I'd bought another one from a well-known high street store. However, the day before we were due to leave, I was informed (in a dedicated bike shop where I knew the proprietor) that this was merely a luggage rack, quite unsuitable for carrying panniers. He advised me to take it back and even offered to lend me his *own* carrier, knowing that I couldn't afford a decent one. I thought it was a very kind offer, and accepted.

The previous week he'd discovered that my bike frame had a kink in it from some big prang in its past. I think he thought I was a bit mad, embarking on this shoestring holiday. This bike had been passed down to me after Pete had grown out of it. It was already second hand when we'd bought it for him. It had drop handlebars and five gears. As it was an average teenage boy's bike, I could only guess what its potted history might be. Anyway I was warned that, with all the weight on, it might crack up if I went down a pothole and I ought not take it to France. But I wouldn't be deterred now. Besides it must have stood up to quite a bit already.

I had bought the boys' panniers and pannier racks as Christmas presents two years earlier, from a catalogue book which allowed me twenty weeks to pay for them. I could just about afford the small weekly amounts for these extras we needed, but I knew it was a more expensive way of buying things and there was less choice to be had. Now I was being told that they were only front panniers. (I'd thought they were

4

a bit on the small side!) Well they'd have to do now. The less room we had, the less weight we could carry.

The *pièce de resistance* had been buying Malc a new bike for his 13th birthday in December (on an extended payment plan from the same club book). It was a black, basic touring bike. He was delighted. But, alas, only seven months later he'd grown too tall for it. We'd raised the seat post and the handlebar stem to their highest limits but still he had to cycle with his knees right up. Luckily, we managed to get an extension for the seat post to rectify this. But now he had to bend right over to reach the handlebars, rather like a Tour de France racer. This caused him some back trouble later on.

Then with only two days left to go, Pete discovered that his back wheel was badly buckled. How could all these things be going wrong now, when we'd spent so much time on planning this holiday? Our cycle-shop friend wasn't able to true the wheel immediately. It wouldn't be ready until today, our departure day. Pete would have to set up his bike at the last minute. He was also given a verbal warning that his wheel might just about see him through this holiday, but then he'd definitely need a new one.

We'd need lights of course. It had been a job to find all the fittings because they'd been put in a safe place. My bike had dynamo lights. However, as my panniers hung low, covering the rear one, I'd need a battery light lower down at the back.

Malc and I had such a laugh putting these lights on the

French side because it meant they were on upside down. The slightest jolt and all the batteries fell out. We had a few repeat performances before putting them on the English side once more.

We'd been advised to take spare light bulbs to France because it wasn't possible to get compatible ones there. We carefully wrapped a couple of spares in toilet paper and tucked them inside a matchbox.

At about 9am Jim and I dropped Pete off at the cycle shop to collect his wheel, then returned to Stroud for last-minute shopping. I took the luggage rack back, hoping for a refund with which I could buy a few more provisions, but I was given a credit note, which annoyed me. There was nothing else I wanted in their shop. I called at the railway station to buy our tickets, then at the Post Office to change my money into francs. It was all happening now.

Tom arrived from the other side of the valley with his bike loaded to the hilt. I don't know how he'd managed to get up Butterrow Hill, either riding or pushing it. When he revealed the contents of his ample panniers to us, we were amazed. Apart from his clothes he had a large saucepan set, a container for a dozen eggs, a larger cooker than ours with its spare gas bottle and an egg poacher – which I used only once because it was impossible to clean.

There was a middle section between his panniers. In it, I spied a leather jacket and a pillow! This was his first attempt at lightweight cycle/camping. We three had tried it briefly the year before, and although we wouldn't be travelling light, we were certainly aiming that way.

I'd decided to take several items of food with us, in the hope that we'd save money. The bulkiest item was four 24-packs of Weetabix. We would each carry a packet. I had an empty shampoo bottle filled with cooking oil. (It had taken me ages to get rid of its perfumey smell). Then there was the empty Biactol bottle (for teenage spots) filled with washing-up liquid. Coffee and sugar were in two plastic beakers with screw-top lids, and I'd filled a little pepper pot with salt. We also had ten packet soups and two packs of spaghetti.

A couple of days before, I had bought two plastic basins and a little camping kettle with a whistle. Now my compact saucepan set wouldn't fit in. Tom offered to carry it for me if I would take his Weetabix.

Being the 'cooking stuff' carrier I had packed socks and tea towels around everything that might rattle.

The previous year I'd been given a roll of brilliantly-bright red cloth. From it I'd made four covers to go over our camping rolls. We'd strap these across the tops of our panniers. They turned out to be a great asset – you could see them a mile away. Pete and Malc each had a tent and a sleeping bag rolled inside theirs, while in mine was a sleeping bag, wrapped around a drumbag containing my clothes. With a dustbin liner underneath these covers, everything would keep dry.

By 1 pm we had the bikes ready to roll, but then we didn't know what to do with our spare time. Jim had checked all the nuts and bolts and there seemed to be nothing left to be done.

Around half past one I decided to cook egg and bacon after all, having dismissed the idea earlier. Rather late to start cooking, but Jim said he'd wash up later. I was just filling in time to appease my nerves.

It started raining. Pete and Tom rushed out to cover their bikes. Goodness knows why, they'd have to stand the rain on holiday.

When it got to 2.30 pm I had no more excuses to hang about. The big moment had arrived and by now I felt quite shaky. What were we letting ourselves in for? We waved cheerio to Jim at the gate and I rode carefully down the lane with my laden bike. The boys came racing by me and I was extremely anxious about them flying down Butterrow Hill, over all the bumps and round the hairpin bends. They hadn't yet got the feel of their loaded bikes. But to my relief, we all met up safely at Stroud station and made our way to the goods crossing at the end of the platform. As no trains were in sight we pushed our bikes across the railway lines. We had about 20 minutes to wait.

Jilly Cooper appeared on the opposite platform and dived straight into the Ladies' Waiting Room. Well, we were almost sure it was her, although she didn't look quite the same as she did on TV (she wasn't smiling so we couldn't see the gap in her front teeth). Whoever it was, she kept popping out to see if the London train was arriving.

A chap came over to us, stinking of booze. He said, "Yes, it *is* Jilly Cooper." (He'd obviously been listening). He added, "I often go drinking with her husband Leo in the Stirrup Cup in Bisley, when she's away in London, of course. I go shooting with him too." I thought it was rather a tall story, although it passed the time as we waited for our train, and diverted my mind from worrying. He also told us he was going up to Sheffield to fetch a lorry and deliver it somewhere for £300. He'd done it all, been everywhere and his sister had cycled all the way to Greece, which made our holiday seem trifling.

The Cheltenham train arrived at last and we grabbed our bikes ready for the great moment. We found the goods van and stood expectantly at the door. I was beginning to feel enthusiastic now.

"YOU CAN'T PUT THOSE BIKES IN HERE!" barked a huge man in uniform who suddenly appeared in the doorway waving his arms about. We stopped dead in our tracks, not believing for a minute what we'd just heard. I got a glimpse of the inside of the goods van as this obnoxious man stood blocking our entrance. There didn't seem to be much in there; just an untidy sprawl of mailbags and one bike. We pleaded, telling him we had a ferry to catch. I was so desperate I took a fiver out of my purse and proffered it. But he would *not* budge. The train was waiting to go; waiting for us to move away from the door. Finally, the whistle blew. Then one by one, the carriages slid by, taking with them our long-planned-for holiday. We stood in utter silence. We were DEVASTATED!

But I couldn't possibly give up now. I'd been dreaming of this holiday for years. I had to do *something*. My adrenalin must have sprung me into action for suddenly, I had a great idea. Leaving the boys frozen to the platform, stunned and silent, I told them I was going to ring home and ask Jim to phone our friend Tony, in Cheltenham. He had a vegetable shop and a big van with a sliding side-door. If he could come and pick us up we might still catch the Plymouth train in Cheltenham.

After I'd phoned home I rushed up to the travel agents where I'd bought the ferry tickets. I wanted to know what would happen if we missed the ferry. I felt that people were looking at me as I ran up the street; I was all red-faced and panicky.

At first, I was told bluntly that we'd lose all our money. Then they decided (as they swirled to face me, relaxed and cross-legged in their ample swivel chairs) that in the circumstances we'd probably be allowed to go the next day, or whenever they had space. Phew!

I returned to the phone box outside the station and rang Jim again. I needed to know if he'd managed to contact Tony yet. He had not. Tony had just left the shop and would be on his way home. Jim said that as soon as he'd spoken to Tony, he'd set off after us and take our panniers in his car. I told him we'd start cycling towards Cheltenham straight away and just hope that he would meet us at some point and pick us up. It was all rather uncertain, but we'd just have to go for it.

The boys were still motionless on the platform. I told them my new plan, whereupon we rushed back over the line and set off like Exocet missiles. The trouble was that Pete, Malc and I were wearing cheap pack-in-the-pocket type flimsy nylon haversacks on our backs. These were full of food and drink to consume on the train and later, on the ferry. Mine was heavy and cut into my armpits.

CHAPTER ONE

I had only reached the first roundabout, just after the railway bridge, when my chain came off and jammed behind the pedal. Pete, who had already reached the next roundabout, happened to look round. He made a complete circle and came back up to me. I felt in a mad panic while he freed the chain. We jumped back on the bikes and caught the others up, pedalling hard. I was at the rear. It was 3.20 pm now and our train was due to leave Cheltenham at 4.42. We had about 15 miles to go, with a long winding incline up through Painswick, then a steep zig-zaggy descent the other side, over the Cotswold edge.

Just as I reached Stratford Park, not yet out of Stroud, the chain came off again for the same reason – panic gear changing. I stopped to put it on. It wasn't jammed this time. Now left behind, I was spurred on by the thought that we might lose our holiday if I didn't do my utmost. I hoped it wouldn't be long before Jim caught me up and took my panniers off me, because I was putting in SO much effort, just as an Olympic athlete might have done. My face, I felt sure, was beetroot red and my heart was thudding. I thought: "I hope I don't have a heart attack!"

I found Malc waiting for me just before Painswick and was extremely grateful. I was almost at breaking point by now. We plodded on upwards and he kept stopping for me to catch up. We were at the highest point before both Jim in his car and Tony in his van arrived - from behind us! No time for questions, we just bundled the rolls and haversacks into the car, ourselves and the bikes into the van, and raced on towards Cheltenham.

Pete and Tom were miles ahead, right down the other side

of the hill near Shurdington, before we picked them up. The four of us stood in the back of the van hanging onto our bikes while Tony drove carefully with his irregular load.

At the station we thanked Tony VERY much. Then the Tannoy announced that the Plymouth train was running 16 minutes late! Maybe, after all, we could have made it by cycling. We had a cup of coffee with Jim in the station café and I tried to relax and get my colour back to normal.

A Cheltenham porter was really helpful and assured us there would be plenty of space on the next train. He couldn't understand why we hadn't been allowed to put our bikes on at Stroud, as there had been another goods van at the back of that train.

The long Plymouth train arrived, with a goods van at both ends and one in the middle. We headed for the central one. It was already quite full but they squeezed our bikes in, telling us that we'd have to take them out again when we reached Bristol, in order for them to get out other luggage at the back. The bikes could go in again afterwards.

We waved cheerio to Jim once more. This time we were *really* off. The train was very crowded but we found four seats at a table and started snacking while we played 'hangman' in an exercise book. When the train stopped at Bristol we dashed down the corridors to the luggage van. But it was the wrong station. We had ten minutes more to go before we reached the main one.

When we arrived at the 'bikes out' station we were told that we must now take them to the empty van at the front of the train. This gave us a bit of a problem as only three of us had come to do the four bikes. Pete had stayed behind to keep our seats and look after the bags. So we flew up the platform with three bikes. The train was so long. In my haste, I'd apparently bumped my wide load on a railway worker's backside as he was bending over to tap the wheels (Malc told me this afterwards). Luckily he'd laughed, but I'm glad I hadn't knocked him over the edge.

Malc put his bike on first and ran back for Pete's. The crowds were thinning and I could see Malc riding hell for leather up the platform. I dawdled around the door to give him more time, but the porters weren't pressuring us, so we needn't have worried. Now our bikes were in an empty luggage van with nothing to tie them up, so we leaned them all at quite an angle and hoped they'd stay there.

We set off through the train to find our carriage again, passing a woman in a wheelchair, the sole diner in the restaurant car. So many people had disembarked at Bristol that there were loads of vacant seats in every carriage. But we decided to stay put. We weren't hemmed in any more.

I thought the boys were being very overcautious to keep going up to check the bikes. Then I discovered that they weren't checking the bikes at all, but the poor woman in the restaurant car. She had some disfiguring complaint that I can't remember the name of. I was really cross with them.

By the time we reached Plymouth we were in high spirits. As we prepared to leave the train, we discovered that a man and youth on the opposite side of the carriage were also going cycling in Brittany. They were a father and son from Dumfries in Scotland who, unlike us, seemed calm and quietly confident. We chatted with them as we lifted our bikes out of the goods van. They weren't camping, so their bikes weren't half so heavy as ours.

After parading up and down the platform with our loaded bikes, we realised how we had to get off. By the lift! We went down one lift, rode under the station, and came up another. It was the wrong side, so we crowded back into the lift with three women and a young girl plus *their* bikes and panniers. What a squeeze! They had gone wrong too. The next time we came up it was the correct side.

I got chatting with them. They were also going to Brittany but were not crossing until 3 pm the next day. Their ages seemed to be 40ish, 30ish, 20ish and 10ish. I kept chatting until I realised that Malc was hopping from one leg to the other, desperate for a loo. I cut short our conversation before he got caught short, and said that perhaps we'd see them around.

We didn't know where to go for the ferry, so decided it must be downhill. This meant crossing a busy flyover then heaving our bikes up an enormous curb. Mine keeled over onto the pavement; I just couldn't hold it. Feeling like a prize idiot, I struggled to heave it upright, with a long queue of people watching me from a nearby bus stop

It wasn't until we were right down the other side that we saw a ferry sign pointing the other way, uphill! We puffed back up this hill, eventually finding the ferry port in the opposite direction.

The port was desolate, but I was grateful to discover some toilets in an obscure car park. We also found a water tap on a tall pipe, sticking oddly out of the tarmac as if it had grown up like a big weed. At last I could get rid of the squash bottle I'd been lugging around. We shared the squash and topped up the bottles from the tap.

It was about 9 pm. The ferry wasn't due to leave until 11.30, so we rode round and round the quays in the dark, filling in time. Pete teased Malc by saying that a certain boat was the ferry. Malc was not sure whether to believe him or not. I worried about producing two child tickets when the time came to get on. The hanging about was becoming unbearable, but it wasn't worth the risk of cycling back into Plymouth.

The main car park began filling up. It was drizzling and as everything had now opened, we went into the terminal building. We loitered in the café area for a while, smelling warm food and watching people tucking in. Our haversack snacks didn't seem quite so appetizing now. Oh well! We left the diners to it and found a space to sit down behind the entrance doors. A while later, we noticed the two 'Scotties' again and kept them in our sights. They seemed to know the ropes, whereas this was all new to us.

There were four people unloading their bikes off a car. They seemed very old to be going on a cycling holiday. I went over to chat to them and discovered they were seasoned cyclists from London.

Now it was time to show our passports; such a casual

affair. We could see cars coming out, so the ferry must have arrived, although we couldn't see it yet. Bikes could go to the front of the queue, so we headed that way. When we saw the ferry Pete was disappointed. It wasn't as big as he thought it would be, in fact, not all that much bigger than the one he'd teased Malc about.

There was a double row of cars behind us, and cars pulling caravans were lining up to our right. Who would go first? We were now in a group with the Scotties and the drizzle was getting wetter. Every time we thought the last vehicle was off, we were disappointed. Where did it put them all?

We joked about which one of us would hand in the tickets, and which two would be half-price. Inwardly, though, I wasn't feeling at all jocular. I handed the tickets to Tom because his peaked cap made him look like an old man (although I wouldn't have dreamt of telling him so!) The Scotties saw the tickets and said, "You don't give those in to get on the ferry. You have to change them at the kiosk for boarding cards."

I raced back through all the parked cars to a kiosk in the car park. The woman exchanged the tickets for four rectangular plastic things and asked, "Where are the rest of you?"

"They're waiting at the front of the queue," I panted. Phew! That was lucky.

We were now getting soaked. But in spite of feeling tired and washed out, I wasn't worrying any more. There were men waving torches about in the dark and the ferry seemed to be empty. The next thing we knew, a whole line of lorries was boarding from our left. We hadn't noticed them. They took ages but at long last it was our turn. We rode up a steep ramp inside and there we just leaned our bikes against a wall.

"Is that it?" I exclaimed. There were ropes all fastened in the wrong places so that we couldn't tie the bikes up properly. The crew gesticulated (they were French). It appeared that we weren't allowed to secure them ourselves – *they* would. We were not at all happy about that, but they were adamant.

Well, we were on, but unfortunately I appeared to have lost the other three and couldn't work the lift. I didn't know which way they'd gone. So I hung around for the Londoners, who were tying up their own bikes and were *not* being told off. There was also a young German lad with a nice bike and a very smart outfit. None of us could work the lift, so we found some stairs instead.

I arrived at an upper deck with rows of seats facing three televisions. The boys were already well established on the front row, looking out for me. But Malc and I couldn't cope with the loudness of the tellies, so we moved further back. However, these seats turned out to be booked, so we returned to the front.

At last the tellies went off. What a relief. Eventually, we settled on the back row, in seats that hadn't been reserved. Lots of people were getting blankets. Some were stretched out on the floor behind us and a few were even lying across several seats.

The engines started. It was hard to tell if we were moving or not so Pete, Malc and I went outside to have a look. The

17

ferry was turning right round and we stayed on deck until the lights of Plymouth had disappeared. Now we were away into the darkness. We went back in and settled down. It felt like a defining moment in my life.

Arrival in France

Roscoff

We had a restless night. It was quite cool, sitting in wet clothes. Closing our eyes, we tried desperately to go to sleep but we just couldn't. Then at about 3 am Tom disappeared. I presumed he'd gone to recline somewhere else, but learned later that he'd been very sick. Yet this was a calm crossing, there was no wind at all. Maybe he shouldn't have had all those *pains au chocolat*.

Malc too felt a bit queasy, in spite of the travel sickness tablets he'd taken. He found the best way to cope was to lie on the floor. Pete and I remained in our seats, stiff and bored. If we sat upright and strained our necks, we could just about see through the windows. I wasn't as tall as Pete, so I had to strain even more. We did this from time to time; for what purpose I don't know, as there was no way we could work out how far we'd been nor how far we still had to go. But it broke the monotony.

After what seemed like an eternity, we noticed a tiny tinge of red on the horizon. Prising ourselves from the seats we walked stiffly out into the chilly darkness. Yes, to our left, the dawn was just breaking, while ahead we could make out the lights of the French coast. I felt a brief flicker of excitement, which lasted half a second. They were so far away that they might as well have been imaginary. The two of us stood there, the only people on deck in the dark. The constant droning of the engines filled our silence. We were shattered. All we craved was sleep.

As we drew nearer, I went back inside to prepare for my grand arrival in this foreign land. In the toilets I splashed cold water onto my face, and oh, what a shock! Was that haggard image staring at me from the mirror really me? I wished I could have hidden my face away.

It took forever to reach those lights on the coast, but at long last the ferry drew into port. Everything looked so grey and desolate; a great anti-climax. Tom and Malc appeared from wherever they had spent half the night, probably looking worse than I did. Tom was still feeling ill. We went back into the lounge and hung around until all the other passengers had gone, not at all keen to disembark. We didn't want to be standing for ages in the fumes below deck. The cleaners were vacuuming all around us when we eventually ventured down. Now we could access our bikes easily and ride straight off.

Whoops - wrong side of the road! After showing our passports we set off towards the town. The sun had risen and there wasn't a cloud in the sky. As we passed through Roscoff I began to fall in love with the town. Nearly all the buildings were of stone. I was entranced by the dark tiles on the steep mansard roofs with their many dormer windows. Already my spirits were rising.

Seeing a camping sign, we followed it, going westward. The countryside looked different from the kind we were used to. There were no hedges, walls or fences to separate the farmland from the road. We passed fields of cabbages, carrots and artichokes; you could almost reach out and touch them. I started to sing 'Savez-vous planter les choux,' until Malc gave me a quizzical look, which made me feel silly. Just a few miles up the road we found a sandy campsite next to a beautiful bay. We were all feeling much more cheerful now and we'd certainly warmed up.

Meandering around the site for a while, just to see what it looked like, we were suddenly accosted by a man emptying dustbins. He looked like a labourer, so we were quite taken aback when he asked to see our passports. He directed us to the office, where we needed to book in.

En route, I smiled at a couple of men who were standing behind a pretty hedge of tamarisk. They smiled back. But, oh, how embarrassed I felt the next day, when I realised what they had been doing - the urinals were the other side of that hedge. Henceforth, whenever I had to visit the office, I resolutely kept my eyes straight ahead.

The highest part of the site seemed best; the grass was short and the ground sandy and dry. Tom plonked himself down on his panniers. He still felt sick. The rest of us began putting up the tents – well, it was mainly Pete, as he was the only one who seemed to have the know how.

But the pegs just wouldn't go in. We kept bending them, and started getting quite hot and cross. Then Malc's hammer broke. (Hadn't Jim said it wouldn't last five minutes?) It was out of his little woodwork set. Malc and I went down to the beach to find a stone that we could hammer with. We managed to pitch one tent fairly well, while the other was up, but ready to flop. We'd run out of pegs. Where could we buy some more?

We tried asking a lady in a nearby tent if there was a camping shop around. She shouted across to someone in a tent the other side of us. In the end the occupants of about four tents were all shouting across to each other. Our heads were going from left to right, trying to follow who was expounding next. It was like watching a tennis match at Wimbledon! After an energetic and heated discussion, where we stood centre stage feeling rather embarrassed, a consensus was reached. It just took them a little while longer to explain it to us. Eventually we understood. There was a big supermarket at St. Pol-de-Léon, a few kilometres the other side of Roscoff.

All these campers seemed to own dogs, but what we'd never seen before were cats on a campsite. There were two here, tethered to long leads.

We set off eastwards to find this supermarket. But after only a mile, Pete's tyre punctured and he was forced to walk all the way back to the campsite. He was really put out.

The rest of us carried on and found the Rallye Supermarché just before St. Pol-de-Léon. Thinking we'd be

View from the campsite near Roscoff on our very first morning

able to shop in here without needing to speak was a myth, because we couldn't find tent pegs anywhere. After consulting our dictionary, I bought two packets of pegs that looked slightly stronger than the ones we'd bent. We returned, borrowed a hammer and soon had the other tent erected.

In our absence Pete had bought us two baguettes from a bread van which came round the site. I heated up two of our packet soups to have with this fresh, crusty bread. It made a tasty snack. At this point I'd visualised us all flopping into bed and having a good sleep. But no - it was such a glorious day and not yet noon, and we were all on a high by now.

We rode back to Roscoff again, for a better look round. Then Tom took Pete to St. Pol to show him the supermarket. When we'd all returned we made our way down to the beach. What a wonderful afternoon. I waded round the bay, up to my thighs in the clear warm water. The sun was beaming down. I felt rejuvenated. Malc explored the rocks while Tom and Pete just larked about in the waves. It was a gorgeous beach, the nicest one I'd ever been on.

In the evening we had another simple meal. I used a whole packet of spaghetti, cooked on Tom's stove, together with a quick-cooking tin of minced meat to go with it, heated up on my stove. I'd also bought a carton of what I'd thought was Dairylea-type cheese, but as I began spreading it onto several slices of our crusty baguette, I realised it was thick yoghurt.

We turned in for the night. I was sharing Malc's tent and Tom was in Pete's. Only then did Malc tell me how he'd got lost in Roscoff earlier that day, after I'd allowed him look round the shops on his own. He told me he'd become completely disorientated, so he had knocked on someone's door (anyone's door) and said in English that he was English and was lost. The woman who'd answered his knocking had fetched her teenage son. He at least could understand Malc a little, although unfortunately, Malc could not understand him. So this lad had cycled out of town with Malc to look for a "campsite near the sea". Our site was the first one they'd come to. I was immensely grateful to the boy, and quite relieved, of course. Also, I thought Malc had acted very sensibly. I, on the other hand, had been rather lax. I shouldn't have left him in the first place.

On our first night in France I hardly slept a wink, even though I'd been awake since 5.30 am the day before. My legs were painfully sore and burned all night. I couldn't bear to lie on them. With the waves lapping round me all afternoon I just hadn't appreciated the strength of the sun's rays. We'd been having such a fabulous time. I hoped the boys weren't sunburnt like me. As far as I could make out they were sound asleep. I didn't hear a peep out of them.

* * * * *

I was first up, which wasn't surprising, after such a long, uncomfortable night. I unzipped the tent as quietly as I could. Outside there was dense mist, not at all inviting. So I wriggled back into my sleeping bag and lay there quietly, not wanting to disturb the boys.

By the time they'd woken up the mist was thinning. I was glad it was still cool because I could wear trousers to cover up my lobster-red legs.

Malc and I were planning to cycle to a little shop we'd heard about at Santec, about two miles further west. First of all though, we needed to practise our French. We spent ages lying on our sleeping bags, reading aloud from Malc's phrase book and making each other laugh. Having done our homework we set off, repeating the phrases in silly tones as we pedalled along.

We found the shop, which was crammed with crates and boxes stacked on top of one another. They'd just had a delivery and we could barely squeeze in. When the shopkeeper started talking to us, we were totally unnerved because we couldn't even see where he was. Eventually we located him but we still hadn't a clue what he was saying. So, very self-consciously, we asked for milk, cheese slices, sultanas and bananas. If we hadn't felt so flummoxed we'd have bought more. This was our first attempt at shopping in a proper shop and even after all that practising we'd blown it. How disappointed we were.

By the time the bread man arrived, ringing his bell, we'd eaten our Weetabix breakfast with bananas, sultanas and milk. Even so, we bought some more crusty baguettes. We found them irresistible.

Pete wasn't having a very good morning. He couldn't find his shorts. He'd looked everywhere. In the end I lent him mine. Luckily they fitted him, as long as he pulled the waist in very tightly with his belt. The three of them went off to ride around the campsite while I cleared up. Without the loads on, cycling had become a more-fun pastime for them.

I was about to take the breakfast dishes to be washed, when Pete returned with a long face. His tyre had punctured *again*. Two punctures in less than 24 hours. That was bad luck.

As I returned, carefully balancing my clean bowls and beakers inside a plastic basin, Pete was just riding off to join the others, having finished his repair. Barely ten minutes later he was back again, FUMING. Yet *another* puncture! This was serious. However, in spite of his frustration, he decided to be really methodical and find out the underlying cause. It was time well spent; a spoke was protruding into the inside of the wheel. We stuck several layers of tape over the end of this sticking-out spoke and hoped it wouldn't pierce the inner tube again. I promised I'd buy him a new tube later on. This one was getting too patched to be trustworthy.

For the first time in ages I had nothing in particular to do. The three boys were happy, pedalling aimlessly around the campsite, finding all the lumps and bumps to ride over. So I used this spare time to give my bike a check over. I re-wound the handlebar tape and adjusted the height and angle of the seat (I'd meant to do these jobs before I left home). There was nowhere to lean the bike, which was a bit of a nuisance, trying to hold it and work on it at the same time. Still, there was no rush.

I watched people working in the nearby fields, packing carrots into boxes and planting cabbages by hand. It was a lovely pastoral scene which reminded me of my childhood back in Lincolnshire. But the soil was quite different here. It looked like dust. I wondered how it could possibly yield all these crops.

With still more time to spare I thought I might as well wash some socks and pants in the washing-up sinks. There seemed to be plenty of hot water. Why waste it? The boys always wore thick, white sports socks, which showed all the dirt and were a devil to dry. They were a devil to wash as well. I'd remembered to bring pegs from home but there was no line. So I spaced the washing down the guy ropes of the tents, hoping the sun would come out. It looked rather like prayer flags in Tibet; a fitting tribute to Dervla Murphy, I thought, who had spent time with Tibetan refugees.

The boys had tired of riding round the site, so they dumped their bikes untidily and ran down to the beach. There was a cool wind blowing so I doubted they'd go for a swim. Pete was wearing my maroon jumper as he'd forgotten to pack his sweatshirt. It wasn't a particularly warm one. The wind blew straight through the loose-knit stitches. Pete didn't seem to be having much luck today.

Ten minutes later they came rushing back. Tom wanted to buy a surfboard. He and Pete jumped on their bikes and rode off at great speed to see what they could find. A little later, Malc and I set off for Roscoff and met them coming back. Tom *had* bought a surfboard. It looked really cumbersome to carry on his bike. As it was inflatable, I couldn't think why he hadn't deflated it.

Apparently, he'd bought a proper surfboard first, without an inkling of how he could carry it. The two boys had spent ages outside the shop, trying to tie it on to the bike with string. But, in the end, Pete was forced to go back into the shop, on Tom's behalf (according to Pete) to explain the problem. The shopkeeper had been good enough to exchange it for this inflatable one, even though they'd scratched it.

Later, Pete decided that he'd quite like one as well. Off they sped again. With Tom's influence, I worried that Pete would blow all his spending money before we'd barely started the holiday. It was obvious that Tom had more to spend than we did.

Meanwhile Malc and I decided to have a better look around Roscoff. If Pete and Tom were spending some of *their* money, we might as well have a treat as well. We went into the Oceanarium. My treat. Inside it was rather dark. The large room was full of huge aquariums containing many varieties of fish. We tried to get interested but found it rather mundane watching fish swimming round and round.

That was until we came to the crabs. A grotesque scene was laid out before us, and I mean 'laid out'. We gasped in disbelief, for lying on its back at the bottom of the tank was a poor crab with only one leg left. Its other legs were strewn all around – broken off. Whatever frightful combat had it been in? It waved its remaining claw about and made pitiful attempts to get up.

When our eyes had adjusted to the darkness we could see more crabs on the rocks above, seemingly poised to pounce on their poor victim again. We couldn't take our eyes off the drama. It was like watching a horror movie, and in that respect, I suppose, we were getting our money's worth, although we did miss out on the action.

What we could have done with now was a cup of coffee (a brandy might have been even better). We went into a nearby café and asked, in French, for coffees. When they arrived we were quite taken aback, because the cups were like eggcups and the coffee was bitterly strong. However, with the generous jug of hot milk provided, we could just about drink it. We made it last for ages; long enough to write five postcards.

Now I thought we should look for the cycle shop. We'd enjoyed walking up and down the touristy streets in the town centre, but what we needed to find were the local people's shops. We unlocked the bikes and did a grand tour of Roscoff's back streets. En route we came across a Spar shop - I'd been unaware that they had Spars here (I shopped in one back home). I'd almost filled a basket with groceries when I suddenly changed my mind. I had to get the inner tube first, for I had no idea what it might cost me. Feeling self-conscious, I went round the shelves, putting everything back in its place. "Nous retournerons plus tard" I said to the shopkeeper as we passed the checkout. I was embarrassed, but pleased with myself for remembering the future tense. The old grey matter must be waking up!

The cycle shop was more like a corrugated shed of a garage with a tiny shop built on to one side. There was an old-fashioned bell on a coiled spring attached to the shop door.

It continued to bounce and jingle long after we'd stepped inside.

They didn't sell tubes in the size Pete had stipulated, but everyone in the shop *and* the garage (for they'd all joined in by now) agreed that we had the right Continental size for the job. I paid 28 francs 50.

Outside, the pavement was barely a foot wide. Your life was in jeopardy when you walked out of the shop. You might get your knees amputated if you weren't careful. Or worse!

Next we found the Post Office, where five stamps cost me 10 francs. Then it was back to the Spar.

Earlier in the day, while Malc and I had been in Santec, Pete had seen the four British women camped down at the bottom end of the site. They'd asked him to invite me round for a chat, and I had taken up their invitation. "Why don't you all come round for some wine tonight?" one of them had suggested. It seemed only fair to make a contribution to the alcohol, even though I had to be careful with my money. Too much spent on one day would mean cutting back the next.

In the Spar they had some really cheap booze. I bought a bottle of wine that cost the equivalent of 70p, and a bottle of cider (60p). I also bought lemonade for the same price as the cider. I spent very little on food. I'd certainly got my priorities right, today.

Pete and Tom had been in the sea on their surfboards, wearing their T-shirts to keep warm. These were now wet, so I had to find room to hang them among my prayer flags.

In the evening we all went down to socialise with the four

Brits and have a drop or two of wine. Joan, the eldest, was the expert; she had a mountaineering tent and a decent bike. The second eldest turned out to be the mother of the other two, although she looked quite young. The girls were called Sophie and Martha. Sophie had just left school. She had a broad Midland accent and permed hair that hung over her eyes like the Old English sheepdog in the Dulux paint advert. She latched on to Pete and Tom and didn't seem able to take her eyes off them, although it was hard to tell with all that hair. They also had a man-friend with a car, in case Martha couldn't stand the pace. The cheats!

We had an enjoyable evening with them in spite of a sudden shower which we had to sit through. Somewhat inebriated, we cycled back to our tents at the top end of the site. It was about 11 pm. We were rather noisy getting in, tripping on the guy ropes in the dark. I should have left the washing out so that we could have seen them.

The bed was really hard, but with the help of the wine I managed, at last, to sleep. The boys went out like lights.

I had meant to phone Jim by now, to let him know we'd arrived safely (albeit two days ago). Joan said she knew the dialling code, but I'd forgotten to get it from her.

CHAPTER THREE

South to Plougastel

We'd decided to pack up camp and move on, taking no particular route. We would just follow our noses and let the holiday evolve. Now that Pete and Tom had their blow-up surfboards to carry, it made sense to be somewhere next to the sea. Malc didn't quite share their enthusiasm for the water.

After studying the map we thought we'd head for Plougastel, a small town below Brest. That way we would head south west from a north-facing coast to a south-facing one, cutting off all the top western corner of Brittany. We couldn't do it all.

There was a lot of packing and clearing up to do. Repacking was much harder than when we'd packed at home. Everything had been so compactly fitted into the panniers to start with, almost like a 3D puzzle. Even then, there had been things that wouldn't fit in. These we had put into our nylon haversacks at the last minute. Now, apart from the fact that we couldn't remember how we'd packed in the first place, we seemed to have more leftovers than ever, which made for bulky haversacks to strap on top of our red rolls.

I stuffed the damp washing into a plastic bag and strapped that on top as well. Malc carried spare trainers in his haversack. He had such big feet (at home we affectionately referred to them as 'planks') that they wouldn't even fit into his panniers (the ones I'd bought by mistake).

Tom did a lot of watching while the rest of us got on with the nitty-gritty. To be fair, though, with those large panniers on his bike, packing was much easier for him. I expect he was bored to death waiting for us. It was 2.30 pm before we were ready to leave and half the day was gone already.

Pete popped over to ask Joan for the dialling code for England. I still hadn't let Jim know we'd arrived! During that brief interlude while we waited for Pete, I noticed that I felt totally different, as though some heavy weight had been lifted from my head – a pressure that I hadn't even been aware of before. I sensed a new feeling of freedom.

Dressed in shorts again (we'd found Pete's) we set off. It was quite sad to be leaving this lovely beach, but we knew we wouldn't see much of Brittany if we stayed in the same place.

We rode westwards to Santec in a fairly sedate fashion, now that our bikes were loaded up again. From there we turned south, heading towards Landivisiau. After riding through a small hamlet called Plougoulm, we reached the D788, which was a main road, although it didn't appear to be very busy. The roads were almost devoid of traffic, just as we'd hoped. We passed old-fashioned farms whose farming methods seemed to be reminiscent of the 1940s and 50s. I could remember old tractors back in England like the ones they were using here.

By the time we reached Berven, still on the main road, we were ready for a break. With the wind in our faces, cycling was proving to be harder than anticipated. We stopped for refreshments, and in the only shop to be found in the village we bought a cakey sort of bread and a jar of Nutella to spread on it. Now we'd need somewhere suitable to sit down. The best place seemed to be in the churchyard.

As we sat there, eating and making crumbs, an old man wearing a cap and slippers came shuffling up to us. He seemed a bit perturbed and kept saying something like "ammer, ammer", pointing to himself then to the church. We hadn't a clue what he was on about, unless he was telling us we shouldn't be eating in the churchyard. However, we continued to do so, feeling rather embarrassed with him watching us. At Tom's instigation, any old man in cap and slippers was now referred to as 'ammer-ammer.'

The church had a rather weird look about it, the architecture being more 'holey' than 'holy' and very ornate. I supposed it was something to do with the Catholics overdoing the decoration!

Berven was on a crossroads. From here we headed due south to Plougouvest. Pete had *another* puncture, but this time it was caused by a nail (for several miles he'd been thinking he had a slow puncture). He didn't fume or curse. By now, he was so used to mending punctures that it was no more trouble than tying his shoelaces. Tom sat and timed him. Pete changed the inner tube and had the panniers back on his bike within seven minutes. I was so glad I'd bought the new tube for him.

Meanwhile, Malc chased a small grocery van up a farm track, but he returned without buying anything; it was all too dear. So far we'd hardly seen any other vehicles between the villages. That is, apart from the occasional scooter which buzzed slowly by, usually ridden by an old man wearing a flat cap, or a plump old lady in dark clothing. In my youth it was Mods and trendy *young* people who raced around on scooters. This was clearly not the case in Brittany.

Along the way, we'd been stopping at nearly every junction for Pete and me to study the map. It seemed as if, the nearer you were to a place, the less likely it was to be signposted. We'd gone wrong quite often. This was tiring when it involved hills, and Brittany was becoming hillier as we progressed inland.

On reaching the outskirts of Landivisiau we skirted the perimeter. Pete, Malc and I were feeling desperately thirsty. Tom had three water bottles, but we three only had one bottle apiece. Ours were empty by now. As we headed away from the town we came across a roadside cafe. While Tom waited outside, we asked the owner if she would mind filling our bottles. Once in there we fancied having a strawberry soda drink each. They were super. I hoped Tom wouldn't feel put out.

It seemed we were going round in circles, unable to orientate ourselves. In a nearby village, where everyone appeared to be watching a wedding, a man gave us directions to Landerneau via a scenic route through La Roche-Maurice. We'd be following the river Elorn. Scenic routes were likely to be hilly ones, although this man assured us that this one wouldn't be. Not by car, I thought, but on a windy day with loaded bikes it was a different matter.

By the time we reached Landerneau we were tired out, but we still had quite a few miles to go. We certainly wouldn't get to Plougastel before dark, let alone find a campsite on the coast below it. I didn't fancy cooking in darkness, so when we passed a little restaurant, I suggested we should have something cheap to eat.

Three of us initially chose pizzas, but as Malc didn't fancy those, we all changed to his choice of omelette and chips. (When in Rome, eat as the English do!) We also had a bottle of cider, which was most enjoyable although it did, perhaps, made us a bit squiffy. Included in the meal was a large basket of bread slices with small packets of butter. Pete pocketed these packets for later use. With all the bread, it was a generous meal. We felt really bloated.

This town, with a river running through the centre, looked beautiful in the evening sun. The shops were tall, terraced buildings, set well back from the river, giving it a very open plan. To me, it was rather like a mini Thames Embankment. Not that I knew London well.

I found that after the food and cider I was more done in than ever and had to walk up *all* the hills. The boys kept stopping for me and even put me at the front to set the pace. I was absolutely shattered.

Eventually, in pitch darkness, we reached Plougastel, which is a small town on a slope somewhere near the Rade de Brest. Now we had to find the coast. We accosted a lady and asked for directions. It was first right, second left, first right and second left. That seemed to be fairly easy to remember. The road was narrow and pot-holey, so we had to be careful. At least *I* tried to be. I had my kinked bike frame to think about! But Tom could never resist taking a downhill slope at full pelt. He sounded like a hurdy-gurdy man, flying over all the bumps. Pete and Malc were somewhere behind him, but I was too preoccupied with my own safety to worry about theirs. We had become accustomed to the open-plan roads. By contrast, the road here was hemmed in with close hedges, rather like those in Devon.

At last we reached the end, where, as far as we could tell in the dark, the road opened out onto a small inlet. There seemed to be some sort of a beach in front of us but we couldn't really be sure. Some distance away to our right, the lights of a bar showed up in the black of night. We cycled over and asked the man behind the bar if there was a campsite. No, there wasn't. He suggested that we might like to camp on the grass by the end of the road.

We rode back to have a look. Peering into the blackness, we found it difficult to see what the ground was like. It appeared to be a wide space with what looked like a big pond behind. But we didn't fancy it; it felt too exposed.

Some distance away to our left, I heard voices from behind a high hedge. I felt sure I'd seen the top of a caravan in a brief moment of moonlight. We pushed the bikes towards it and found a gap in the hedge. A steep, narrow path led between the bushes. It was difficult forcing our heavy bikes through, with slippery gravel underfoot. Now we were in a long sloping field and could make out several old-fashioned caravans close by, while lower down there seemed to be a cluster of tents.

We hadn't a clue what this place was but were quite relieved to find it. It felt much safer to be near civilization at this time of night. It was buzzing with noise. Kids were milling about everywhere. Perhaps they would know where I could find a telephone. I felt I really must try to ring Jim.

Pete started putting up his tent. Tom sat on his panniers and held a torch for him but after a while got bored and disappeared. We discovered later that he'd gone all the way back to the bar and bought at least five chocolate bars. Abandoned in the dark to erect this shared tent, Pete was furious.

We'd decided the previous night that from now on we'd pitch our two little tents in a line, with the flysheet in between to connect them. This way we could call it one tent and be charged accordingly. We'd felt somewhat miffed that people with a huge tent were paying the same price as we did for a small one. Goodness knows why we were bothering to do this now, but Malc was waiting for Pete to finish his tent so that he could get the exact width to put the flysheet between the two.

Meanwhile, three giggling girls led me along a little back lane to a pub-type place emitting very loud music. They thought I might be able to ring up from there. Although there wasn't a public phone, the proprietors found out how much it would cost per minute and allowed me to use their own phone. I tried Joan's code, without success. A lady behind the bar was most helpful and looked up another code. However, it was so noisy in there with the Communards blaring out that they asked me into a back room. Here, a polite young man who spoke a little English tried to help me. (There was a large mirror behind the phone and I was flabbergasted to see how dreadful I looked in it – my hair was all straggly and my nose, cheeks and chin were bright red.) He found other codes and we tried them, but they didn't work either. Even the man running the disco tried, in between putting on records (which were all British and American pop hits from two years earlier) but no luck!

Now I was worried that Jim might be getting anxious about us. As I made my way back along the lane, young teenagers were to-ing and fro-ing between the campsite and the disco, asking me for cigarettes as they passed by.

Fumbling and struggling in the dark, Malc and I finished putting up our tent. Pete sat nearby. I could sense he was still angry.

Around 11 pm we went up to the disco place to use their facilities and fill our water bottles. It was a disturbed night for us, with strong wind and heavy rain from time to time. We were convinced that someone was messing about with our bikes (when it's windy you can imagine all sorts of things are happening out there). We'd left the panniers on the bikes because it seemed improbable we'd stay here another night. There was no shop, toilet or water tap. But we hoped nothing would get nicked. Again my legs were burnt, but this time with the wind. It was SO uncomfortable lying on that silly, skimpy camping mat. Last year, when we'd had a brief practice run, we'd used some cheap plastic, inflatable mattresses. They'd been rather heavy to carry, took forever to blow up and even longer to deflate, but oh boy, did I sleep.

* * * * *

Pete, Malc and I were becoming more and more annoyed with Tom; he wasn't pulling his weight. So instead of leaving him slumbering in his cosy cocoon while we did the chores, we woke him up. He wasn't very pleased. However, it was impossible to *make* him help us and in the end, Malc and I took down the tents. Pete spent ages tightening his panniers and fiddling with his bike – a ploy of Tom's. We'd had no breakfast. We weren't starving (otherwise we'd have eaten dry Weetabix), just gnawingly empty. Tom kept covertly nibbling his chocolate bars, but he didn't offer any to us.

It was a problem to know where to prop the bikes, ready to load them. As there were two unoccupied caravans close by, we leaned them against the nearest one. No sooner had we done so than a car full of people appeared and parked between these two caravans. Which one was theirs? We rushed over to remove the bikes quickly, but luckily the new arrivals went into the farther caravan. So we leaned them back again and carried on taking down the tents.

The inside of the car seemed to be squirming with kids

and dogs. When we next looked over, we were surprised to see a teenage girl putting two little boys and a toddler into an empty pram-chassis. The toddler was placed at the front with the other two squeezed in behind him. When they were safely squashed in, she let go of the chassis – downhill, heading straight towards their caravan.

BANG! It hit the side of the van with a loud thud, jolting the three little boys alarmingly. They squealed with delight. It was so hair-raising that we sat shocked and speechless. She repeated this spectacle over and over again. Each time we held our breath, waiting for the big bang. But we ended up laughing with them. They didn't seem to be hurt. The two boys had such comical, chubby faces and wore enormous round glasses. The middle one we named Benny Hill, after the comedian. The resemblance was astonishing.

Eventually we went back to the job in hand, feeling much more light-hearted. But our task proved to be almost impossible now, because their three dogs had been let loose and began to hassle us. The smallest one, a female that was more like a large kitten than a dog, ran up and pounced onto our tents as we tried to flatten them. The other two, which were male, chased after her, making a complete hash of our tent-rolling efforts. One of the dogs was like a huge black wolf. We didn't want to mess with him. It was so funny, though. We couldn't be cross. The mother, peeling potatoes, managed a smile, but only a small one.

At last we were ready to go. The mother gave us another

smile and an "au revoir" as we passed by her, pushing our bikes towards the hole in the hedge.

When we saw the bay in daylight there was no beach at all – just a load of rocks and seaweed. Masses of people, young and old, were bent over, hard at work on the rocks; but what work we couldn't tell. We surmised that they were harvesting mussels or something. Perhaps the campsite was a place for mussel gatherers to stay. As we cycled by, they raised their heads to stare at us. When we turned the corner and looked back, they were still staring.

We puffed up the long winding road to Plougastel in our usual order: Pete first, Tom close on his tail, followed by Malc and with me bringing up the rear. We passed many fields of strawberries and I recalled seeing 'Fraises de Plougastel' in the Roscoff shops. They were obviously very prized strawberries, as in one field I saw electric wires running down each row. We also passed field after field of sweetcorn, artichokes and cabbages. What a productive farming area this was.

It was surprising to see the town of Plougastel bursting with life, as this was a Sunday morning. We'd expected it to be quiet, as in England. A coach drew into the square and out of the door streamed a line of wrinkly old witches in long black dresses. They wore tall black, lacy hats with black ribbons hanging down onto their cheeks. We just couldn't believe our eyes. Were we seeing things? It was all so bizarre. Then we decided that this must be their Sunday best.

There was a stall selling fruit in the market square. I bought eight bananas and eight peaches but with my arms so full of fruit I found myself struggling to hold the bike. Malc and I ate our share straight away, drooling peach juice down our chins. I had my bike propped against the market stall and sensed that the weight of it was wobbling the trestles a bit. I hoped the stallholder wouldn't notice.

Pete and Tom came out of a supermarket with something else to eat - they didn't fancy the fruit I'd bought them. I persuaded them to carry their own bananas, but they wouldn't carry the peaches as well. So with difficulty, I stuffed these into the little side-pockets of my panniers. For a treat, Malc and I bought some orange juice. So far, we'd only had water in our bottles, but the free camping had allowed us extra money for a treat. Tom and Pete bought grape juice.

Right! We must get going and find a decent beach, then the boys could do some more surfing. (Well, not proper surfing, of course. You couldn't stand up on these inflated toys.)

We cycled eastwards out of town hoping to find a good beach further south. But because of the rugged nature of the coastline, we had to travel in a big arc.

Before long it began to pour with rain. We stood against a high hedge to put our anoraks on. Tom's was new and very waterproof, whereas our anoraks, bought from Stroud's Shambles market (second-hand) proved to be only semi-waterproof, even though they bore the Peter Storm label.

It was a heavy burst of rain and as soon as it eased slightly we decided to get cycling, hoping for the best. However, another shower soon followed. This time it was absolutely torrential. We became so wet that there was no point in sheltering, although we stopped briefly to take a photo of the road, which had turned into a fast-flowing river. The pelting rain hurt our faces but we battled on with heads down and eyes screwed up.

At last it relented. We pedalled on, through Lopheret and Daoulas, hoping that we'd dry off. There were ominous distant rumbles of thunder all around us, but we couldn't see any lightning.

Then, within minutes, the sky had closed in on us, black as night. Now we were in for it! Lightning was zig-zagging down to every corner of the earth. The thunder cracked and crashed deafeningly around us. It felt as if all the heavens were shaking. There was just nowhere to hide. We were frightened to death. Never had we experienced a storm of such ferocity and all we could do was keep our heads down once again and bravely plough on. The lightning lit our way through the darkness as our wheels made furrows through the cascading waters.

When we reached the next town, Hôpital Camfrout, the road became miraculously dry. Out came the sun and we began to steam. Hurray! We felt bonded together like soldiers who have just won a battle.

There were no shops or cafés to be seen, so we carried on, pedalling at a good pace down the D770, feeling euphoric. But we were brought up sharply when the road came to an abrupt end. A newly-constructed motorway had been built across it. As yet it was traffic-free, the surfacing not yet completed. It wasn't on our map and we didn't fancy riding on it, for who knows where it might have led us?

Well, we'd stopped now, so we sat in a layby and ate a huge bag of crisps and rested. I ate one of the peaches, which I'd accidentally squashed by throwing my bike down onto the verge. While Pete picked blackberries, Tom hogged the crisps and Malc pinched some fluorescent ribbon off the roadworks, believing it might come in handy.

We back-tracked up the road, taking the first turning to the left onto the coastal road to Le Faou. Malc's brakes were rubbing on the wheel, so we stopped for Pete to adjust them. A little later we stopped again so that Pete could realign my dynamo. I'd knocked it out of place when I'd slung my bike down. Being so waterlogged, it was difficult getting on and off our bikes. But riding kept us warm.

Le Faou was a lovely old place; at least it was to us, seeming like a dry oasis in the midst of water. We dismounted and squelched around, straight legged. I wanted to take a photo of the town, but the buildings were too close together to get enough into view. Tom had the same problem, so he took a photo of a snazzy motorbike instead.

We each went our own way to look for a toilet. Pete found one at the back of a posh restaurant where English people were dining, while Tom and Malc found something more primitive. Mine was a proper English-type toilet with a seat and a flush. It was signposted just inside the entrance to a bar, thank goodness! It meant I could sneak in without having to ask anyone - I felt such a freak and my sodden plimsolls were making noises like cowpats falling. I slipped in and out unnoticed.

With chocolate to help us on our way we eased ourselves back onto the bikes. I realised that I was enjoying today's cycling more than yesterday's, in spite of the horrendous weather.

After Le Faou the rain began again. This time it was just the normal sort of rain, but it went on and on and on. There was no point in stopping; we were wet to the skin. If we stood on the pedals the water gushed down our legs and out into our shoes. It was a peculiar sensation. I tried it several times when the water built up inside my trousers. The traffic had increased and we needed to take great care to avoid wobbling. Cars whizzed by on our left, showering our legs with even more water. But the scenery on the right made up for it; it was absolutely beautiful – almost like mini-fjords, with all the ins and outs of the coastline.

Pete and Tom were well ahead, racing downhill, while Malc and I held back. Suddenly we saw a formidable right-hand bend going over a huge bridge. We panicked and managed to make an emergency stop in the nick of time. By great fortune there was a car park just before the bridge. Dragging our feet along the ground to assist the wet brakes, we skidded along its whole length, eventually coming to a halt before hitting the wire fence at the far end. Goodness knows what we'd have done without this space to stop!

Pete and Tom were nowhere to be seen. They had disappeared completely. With immense relief, we found them halfway along the bridge. How on earth had they negotiated that sharp bend at the speed they had been going? This bridge was the Pont de Térénez, spanning the river Aulne, which was way down below us. Far beneath, we could see people walking along the riverside, looking minuscule. Pete and Tom were dropping the little butter packets off the bridge, trying to hit them (they'd gone off a bit anyway – the butter not the people!) In retrospect I hoped the boys hadn't injured anyone. I didn't think to chide them. I was so happy to find them alive, they could have done anything.

The sun came out and we took photos of the wonderful panorama from the bridge. The river wound its way into the distance towards the sea, with the dark Forêt de Landévennec covering the hills on its left.

The road ahead inclined steeply. As we were worn out by now, we delayed cycling for quite a while. Even then Malc and I didn't have much energy. After just a few pushes on the pedals we got off to walk. We were boiling. Tom took a photo of us both struggling up the hill, steaming like kettles. He and Pete had already reached the top.

The rest of the journey was not too complicated. It was very up and down, but the sort of up and down where, if you go fast enough downhill, you can almost reach the crown of the next hill without too much pedalling. At one point we backtracked to find a route to Telgruc-sur-Mer – a small town which wasn't, in fact, on the sea at all, but two miles inland. We gave it a miss after all and returned to the coastal road, whizzing down the next hill, where we found a campsite.

Looking down over the rocks we were quite disappointed with the beach – there wasn't one. (We didn't realise at the time that the tide was right in.) Nevertheless, I went into the site office and bought eggs, potatoes, bread and milk and, of course, postcards. I could never resist them. But we didn't book in.

The lady in there kindly looked up the dialling code for England. It turned out to be the one I'd been given before. Malc named this poor woman 'Madame Duck' because she had a deformed spine which made her lean over at right-angles and waddle as she walked. She was, in fact, very pretty with kind blue eyes and a really pleasant manner, and seemed to have no hang-ups at all about her disability. It was Malc who had the shortcomings, but he would grow out of them, hopefully.

Pete and Tom offered to carry on over the peninsula to check out the next bay. They pedalled off enthusiastically, seeming to have much more energy than Malc and me. They soon returned, with the news that the next bay was better. So on we went again, up and down the picturesque coastline, with me now carrying heavy groceries in my nylon haversack. The next bay was all rocks and caves. It turned out that the two boys hadn't actually found a better bay, at all. They'd just assumed that there would be one – soon. This fact niggled Malc. He thought we were going on a wild goose chase and he'd had enough for one day.

Halfway down a hill we found an isolated phone box. I shouted to the boys that I was stopping. They actually heard me and waited while I tried, yet again, to phone Jim. Still no luck! I ought to have let him know by now that we were OK. I felt quite guilty, especially as I was enjoying myself so much.

Pete greets me as I arrive on Le Pont de Térénez in the rain

We carried on down the long descent. Before reaching the bottom, Malc and I were stopped by two small children. They had rescued two of Tom's water bottles when they had flown out of his panniers as he careered downhill. He was always losing things in this way. Once he had lost his sunglasses three times in succession. It's a good job we were always behind him.

An English family in a brown Mini came past and waved enthusiastically. They obviously saw some form of British identity about us – maybe the Brittany Ferries stickers on our handlebar bags.

As we rode over the brow of the next hill we all gasped "Wow!" A magnificent stretch of sand came into view. This was Pentrez Plage, with a beach stretching for at least two miles. A road ran along its whole length. At our end there was a small travelling fair next to the beach. It seemed to be a lively and inviting place.

We found lots of campsites, one after another. The third one was slightly cheaper than the first two, so we chose that one and booked a plot for *one* tent.

From the bottom of our anoraks downwards, our trousers were now bone dry. Underneath, though, we were steaming wet, like racehorses after the Gold Cup. All of our belongings in the back panniers were dry, where everything had been wrapped in plastic bags. But it was a different matter with our front, handlebar bags. They were soaked. I'd bought Malc's and mine from the Club book. They were red with 'Velo' written across the front and looked quite natty. In fact, they were cheap and flimsy. Jim had made cardboard stiffeners for them which he'd varnished carefully on both sides, to make them waterproof. Unfortunately, these were all floppy now.

We assessed the damage. Pete's book on bike repairs and his French phrase book were soaked; so were Malc's school vocabulary book and his and Tom's diaries - all the lines had washed away. We eventually used Tom's for toilet paper when our supply ran out! He wasn't making notes in it anyway. Luckily, I kept my diary in a little plastic bag.

Tom and I put up the tents, as I was determined that he was not going to get away scot free. We had to make it look like a single tent but we didn't have the same knack as Pete and Malc. Then I peeled and boiled a load of potatoes which we ate with a tin of minced meat of some sort, from the camp shop. For pudding we stuffed ourselves with a large packet of biscuits – big round ones with chocolate in the middle (but not a patch on English biscuits).

I was overwhelmed by the quantity of wet clothes that would need drying, but the priority was to get into dry beds. When Malc took off his trainers, his feet looked like cauliflowers, all white and shrivelled. For ages, he couldn't bear to walk on them.

It was a good end to a challenging day. I was looking forward to a decent night's sleep to catch up on what I'd missed. Tonight I had no sunburn, no windburn and was quite tired. But, unbelievably, I had an ingrowing toenail which niggled me nearly all night long, presumably from wearing those wet plimsolls all day. I could have cried – not just from the discomfort but the frustration of not being able to sleep. To add to my difficulties, in the still of the night, the sea sounded like a roaring express engine, coming and going like the waves themselves.

CHAPTER FOUR

Sea, sun and sand

Pentrez Plage, Baie de Douarnenez

For most of the day, Pete and Tom kept going into the sea with their surfboards. They'd come back frequently to warm up. A cool northerly wind was blowing, although it was sunny. Each time they returned, Tom would change into another T-shirt. After he'd done this about three times, I began to get quite annoyed. I was already overwhelmed with clothes that needed drying. There was still the bag of washed clothes from Roscoff. They'd gone all smelly now and would have to be re-washed. My priority, however, was to get yesterday's clothes dry, plus the towels that were in constant use.

Malc wished he'd bought an inflatable surfboard as the others were having so much fun with theirs. On the other hand, he was worried about going back into the sea as he reckoned a crab had nipped him. I allowed him to wear his old trainers in the water. I didn't want him to miss out, bless his (great big) cotton socks.

Pete somehow acquired several punctures in his surfboard. I walked up to the shop at the very top of the campsite to see what I could buy to repair it with. My toe was still hurting and it was quite a distance uphill, past countless camping plots as big as fields, then alongside the farm to a gate at the top. The walk was worth it though, because I found a suitable repair kit (using much sign language – and money!)

In the afternoon, Malc and I rode around the immediate area to look for shops selling inflatable surfboards. There were no other shops, let alone surfboards.

I couldn't be bothered to go to the beach. I wasn't feeling very well. Being run down from lack of sleep seemed to have brought out my perennial weakness – a sore throat and swollen glands.

While checking to see how his phrase book was drying out, Pete rediscovered his original dialling code for England. I found a phone box and managed, at last, to get through. I realised what I'd been doing wrong most the time – I needed to put at least 10 francs (£1) in first! Anyway, Jim didn't sound as if he'd been worried at all.

For some reason, it was a noisy night on the campsite. People were coming and going until at least four in the morning. Malc and I lay listening. We worried that our bikes might get stolen. Twice I got out of my sleeping bag to see what was going on, peering from under the flysheet. I saw a couple of men going up and down with torches, shining them all around. In the dark, it was hard to make out what they were up to. Next morning, there were a few broken bottles outside the washrooms; otherwise everything seemed OK – except that Malc and I had been deprived of sleep. Pete and Tom had slept through it all.

* * * * *

Pete suggested that I should use the camp washing machine, so first thing in the morning I went up to the office to buy a *jeton* (token) to operate it with. Meanwhile Pete set off to locate the laundry room and found it was all locked up. Back in the office the girl couldn't find a key for it anywhere, so I couldn't use the machine after all. Feeling miffed, I got my money back and walked all the way up to the shop to buy some Ariel. A washing machine would have saved me a lot of time. Never mind! At least the toe felt a bit easier.

My first job would be to re-wash the even more smelly clothes from Roscoff. I immersed the socks and pants into a sink full of lovely hot, soapy water, working up a sweat as I pummelled and squeezed out the smell. When they were all done and rinsed I filled the sink with suds again and tackled the next load. During this prolonged session, quite a few women came to do their washing up. I tried conversing with some of them, but didn't have much luck. In retrospect, they probably didn't approve of me washing clothes in the washing-up sinks.

Meanwhile Pete had fixed up two washing lines for me at either end of the tent and tied them to the hedge. It was such a relief to be able to hang the washing out properly.

Tom never got up early enough to fetch the milk or to eat breakfast with us, so it peeved us when we witnessed him putting *six* Weetabix into his dish. He then took much more than his fair share of milk and sultanas. We watched in disbelief. I vowed to ration him a bit, if I could. From then on, we began hiding food in Malc's tent so that we'd have some left for later, instead of Tom pigging it all in one go. I trusted my boys not to help themselves before asking first. They knew well the constraints of making ends meet.

Malc and I decided we'd cycle over to Telgruc later on, to look for a surfboard. Pete and Tom continued in the same manner as the day before, but they seemed to spend less time in the sea and more time sunbathing outside the tent – sitting on the surfboards and peeling skin off their bodies! In spite of using sun tan lotion, they'd got quite burnt from spending so much time in the sea. Tom had a great soggy blister where he normally wore his watch.

We had a snacky lunch again – mainly crisps (which we bought in huge packets on the site), baguettes and biscuits. We'd been chomping through the Weetabix for breakfast, so gradually there would be more spare room in our panniers. That would be sooner rather than later, if Tom had anything to do with it!

In the early afternoon Malc and I set off for Telgruc, about six miles away up the 'roller coaster' coast line. The shops were closed for lunch, so we rode around town for half an hour, waiting for the 2.30 pm re-opening time. The brown Mini was in the square. So was the Englishman. He was surrounded by a crowd of French teenagers and looked very amused. They were taking turns to sing him English songs like 'Baa Baa Black Sheep'!

In a town as small as Telgruc we were lucky to find a shop

which sold almost everything, including inflatable surfboards. Now, at last, Malc could join in with Pete and Tom and have some fun in the sea.

While we'd been meandering round the streets, we'd discovered a supermarket. It was tucked away in a quiet little corner, as if the locals were trying to hide it from view. We returned there afterwards and stocked up. It was high time we had something different to eat, so I bought two tins of ravioli for that night, and a huge tin of mutton and bean cassoulet (something I'd never come across before), plus a tin of ratatouille for the next night. I also bought vermicelli, another novelty. It looked as if it would cook very quickly.

We were delighted to find a quicker inland route back to the site; almost like a Roman road and with far fewer inclines. It brought us directly to our shop at the top of the campsite. All we had to do then was wheel our bikes down through the gate. Piece of cake.

That night we had ravioli and vermicelli. Tom wasn't keen on the latter but ate it nevertheless. I hadn't bothered to go on the beach again as I still felt below par, but at least I dropped off to sleep - eventually.

* * * * *

In the early hours of the morning, I awoke to find a gale blowing. At one stage I found myself hanging on to the tent pole to steady it. The rain was coming in on the windward side and my sleeping bag was getting wet. Pete was in a similar predicament in his tent. His sleeping bag was wet. There was nothing for it but to get up.

Pete crawled through the 'inner sanctum' into our tent. Malc was annoyed. He could have carried on dozing, but I made him get up. The three of us needed to sit on his side of the tent to keep dry. We sat there, scrunched up, glumly listening to the wind and rain, with our feet facing the puddles that were now forming on the ground sheet. Tom slept through it all.

The rain had stopped by the time the shop would be opening. Pete went to buy some milk and we ate our breakfast on the dry side of the tent. As an extra treat we had some cakey-bread spread with Nutella, saved from the day before (then we hid it again).

After the storm it was a beautiful day, so I said, "Blow Tom. Why should we hang around waiting for him to have his breakfast?" We went off for a walk along the beach, leaving him a quarter of the milk and a quarter of the sultanas.

We just walked and walked, with the sea on our right and the sun on our left. There were land yachts out on the sand making the most of the strong breeze. We'd never seen them before. A land yacht seemed to us to be more like a racing car than a boat, with a triangular sail on top, although as they were driven by one person in a recumbent position they looked somewhat like sledges on wheels. They tore up and down the whole length of the beach, their tyres swishing on the sand as they raced by, their sails billowing in the wind. They were probably cursing us for being in their way.

At the end of the bay we discovered rocky cliffs with lots

of small caves and rock pools. We spent ages exploring, finding weird creatures in the pools and generally having a great time. Here there was shelter from the cool wind, and Pete had warmed up. The breeze had been blowing straight through the jumper he was still borrowing from me.

How content we were! We could have stayed there all day, but by now my conscience was pricking me. I thought of Tom sitting around for hours, wondering where we were, feeling abandoned. So reluctantly we made our slow return, with the sun now hot on our backs. It was well after midday when we arrived at the site. Tom *was* sitting there waiting, but he'd only *just* got up and was hoping someone might find his wash-bag for him because he couldn't.

In the afternoon we all frolicked in the sea, any hard feelings between us now forgotten. Malc's inflatable wasn't as big as those of Pete and Tom and it didn't hold him up so high in the water, even though it had cost more! No matter. Now he could join in with the other two and forget about what might be lurking in the water, waiting to bite him. We splashed, swam and larked about for ages, having a whale of a time. We were making the most of this beautiful bay, for tomorrow we planned to move on south, to Concarneau.

That night we had our lovely meal of mutton cassoulet, ratatouille and vermicelli (with potatoes for Tom) cooked in two double saucepans and on two cookers.

Later that evening, while the boys were gaily riding round the campsite, Pete skidded into a deep pothole. His rear wheel buckled like a banana. He dragged the bike back up to the tent, looking distraught. Pathetically, we felt near to tears, not knowing what to do next. Then we remembered a couple of cyclists we'd seen, camped further up the site. We went to find them. Perhaps they could offer us some advice. They turned out to be Swiss and luckily, spoke quite a bit of English. Our best bet, they said, was to go to Quimper, the main city, about 30 kilometres away. They knew of a big cycle shop near the railway station. Pete and I resolved to hitchhike there the next day, although we dreaded the thought of doing so.

There was a Belgian chap, whom we liked immensely, who was camped two plots up from us. Whenever he passed by, he'd wave and greet us. Now he could see we were in trouble and came to find out what the problem was. After examining the wheel carefully, he told us it *could* be straightened out, but it would need clamping. He had all the necessary tools – back home!

* * * * *

It was 10.30 am before Pete and I were ready to go. I left the train and ferry tickets, together with the travellers' cheques, hidden in the bedding. These were to enable Malc and Tom to get home, in case anything should happen to us. (I'm not a very brave or optimistic hitchhiker!)

Before we set off, we thought we'd ask the girl in the camp office if she knew of anyone who might be driving to Quimper. Her cyclist boyfriend was in there. They both agreed that there was no need to go all the way to Quimper. There was a good cycle shop in Châtaulin, which was only 13 kilometres away. That wouldn't be so bad.

We set off, walking the whole length of the little coastal road, right to the end of the bay. Here at last, we managed to get a lift with a pleasant elderly couple who were from Paris. Unfortunately, they couldn't take us any further than the main road. While we were getting out of their car, a young woman drew up whom they knew. They asked her if *she* could take us to Châtaulin. But alas, she couldn't. Although she was going there, she had to pick up loads of children. There wouldn't be room for us all. What a shame!

So on we walked, on and on, with the sun beating down on us. We were roasting. It was the hottest day of our holiday and we were wearing trousers. The drivers who passed us pretended we weren't there, or perhaps they were looking down their noses at us. Maybe we did look a bit scruffy. Pete was constantly banging the spindle of his wheel onto his leg, which he found extremely irritating and rather painful.

We continued up and up, into the middle of nowhere. The scenery was gorgeous and the verges full of cornflowers and heather. We could still see the bay far back below us, glinting in the sun. As we got higher we saw lots of dead trees and wondered what might be killing them.

On reaching a roundabout onto a busier road, we thought this would be it. Someone was bound to pick us up now. But no! We were almost in sight of Châtaulin before we struck lucky. The driver who picked us up said he was Belgian. He was very friendly; so was his dog. I sat in the back with it.

Like its owner it was large with lots of curly white hair. It would *not* leave me alone. It was just like being molested by Rod Hull's puppet Emu. It wouldn't keep still for one moment, wriggling, slobbering and biting, though in a most friendly manner. I was thoroughly worn out with its constant attentiveness.

The Belgian was as chatty as his dog was 'kissy' but we were very grateful to him for the lift. We'd been so hot and tired. He dropped us off outside the cycle shop on the main road into Châtaulin. But it was closed. There was more than half an hour to wait before opening time, so we walked on round the corner and into town.

What a beautiful place! Running through the middle was a wide river, spanned by several bridges. Each bridge was festooned with brightly-coloured flowers – baskets of cascading busy lizzies and geraniums. It was absolutely charming. As in Landerneau, the buildings were set well back from the river, allowing lots of open space in the town centre.

It was market day. Pete and I treated ourselves to some fruit, but not before I'd found a tap to wash off all the dogginess from my face and arms. Next I found a bank to change money into francs. This was from my emergency fund (money that I'd saved to pay the telephone bill back home!) In the exchange I received only £17 worth for my £20.

We returned to the cycle shop. It was a double-fronted property with an alleyway down the middle leading into a garage.

The proprietress arrived, rather flustered. In one hand, she was weighed down with a sleeping baby in a carrycot, while her other was clutching the small hand of a chubby and reluctant little girl. She unlocked the two shops on either side of the alley and placed the carrycot on the floor of the shop on the left. She then came to serve us in the opposite shop.

With the whining, thumb-sucking girl clinging onto the back of her skirt, the lady applied many different gadgets to Pete's bent wheel, trying to remove the gears. We needed this gear block to be fitted onto a new wheel. Although the shop appeared to be very well equipped, they didn't have the necessary tool for the job. After many attempts she apologised for failing us. We were equally sorry but grateful to her for all the time and effort she had given. We paid for a new wheel and departed, not really knowing what we were going do with it. I carried this one. Now we each had a spindle to bang onto our legs!

We thought we ought to look for a supermarket to buy food for Tom and Malc. But, being half-hearted in our search, we only scoured the middle of town and couldn't find a food shop anywhere. We ended up buying just a small amount of fruit from the market.

We'd walked right out of town before we realised that I'd left Pete's phrase book on the shop counter. Pete went back for it, which was very magnanimous of him, seeing that it was *I* who'd forgotten it. He was tired though and showed it by dawdling all the way, dragging his feet. I wished I'd gone instead. I sat on the pavement, watching all the potential lifts whizzing by.

After plodding for about a mile along the hot tarmac we

were picked up by a couple with a young son. Because of our language difficulties and the fact that Pentrez Plage was south of the direct route, we told them we were heading for Crozon, a town that lay straight ahead, along this main road. It would be simple enough, we thought, to stop them at the appropriate junction and thumb another lift south, to Pentrez Plage.

We sat in awkward silence most of the way, mainly because we were looking out for our junction but also because we couldn't think of anything to say. We were fed up and worn out. The poor little boy, squashed in the back with us, didn't know where to look. He found it all so embarrassing.

About five miles along the main road they stopped just before a junction and dropped us off. We were puzzled. This *was* our junction but we hadn't even asked them to stop yet. We'd assumed they were continuing to Crozon and, of course, they thought *we* were!

So, suspecting that they might now turn left towards the coast, we rushed across the road, before they'd even had time to negotiate the roundabout (the French way round!) As they turned south off the roundabout, they were surprised to see us waiting there. They stopped to pick us up again, realising we were all going the same way after all. It was quite funny really but we hardly managed a smile between us.

Then, by a great stroke of luck, they drove right to the beach at Pentrez Plage and dropped us off just a few yards from our campsite. Pete and I thanked them gratefully.

Now Pete had to get the block off his old wheel. He took

out all his tools but, needless to say, he had nothing that fitted either. The Belgian chap came past with his four kids who were struggling to carry their boat up the track. He shouted over and promised he'd be right back to see if he could help. He returned with a hammer and various other tools and tried all sorts of methods. Nothing worked. Again, he told us he had all the tools back in Belgium. He *so* wanted to help us. We could see ourselves stuck there forever.

It was now about 7 pm, and our only hope was to go to an old garage Malc and I had passed on the Roman road, on our return from Telgruc. It was in a little place called St. Nic, about two miles away. We'd seen an assortment of second-hand bikes for sale, propped against the wall. The boys hurriedly strapped the two wheels to Tom's bike and with Pete riding mine, they dashed off to get there before closing time at 7.30 pm.

I strolled up to the shop at the top, feeling exhausted and headachey from the heat and frustration of the day. Here I browsed leisurely round the store, looking for something both cheap and nourishing for our supper.

The instant I stepped out of the doorway the three boys came flying past, startling me. Pete made a spectacular pit stop to tell me the good news – the mechanic had changed the gears over free of charge. Not only that, we could have bought the wheel there too!

While I cooked a meal, Pete reassembled his bike. We were feeling much happier now. Just as I was dishing up, a couple arrived on bikes, looking for a space to camp. When they saw all our tools they rushed over to ask if they could borrow some, once they'd put up their tent. They were from Staffordshire, they told us. Liz was a physiotherapist and Ian a PE teacher. They looked to be in their late twenties and we warmed to them immediately.

Later, outside our tent, Ian put new brake-blocks onto Liz's bike. It had the rustiest wheels imaginable but was otherwise almost reasonable. When he'd finished leaning over the bike he found he couldn't get up. His back had crocked out. Liz got him down onto his stomach and began massaging him and giving him exercises to do. Next morning I saw him in the tent. He was still on his hands and knees. So much for Liz's expertise!

We were planning to move on to Concarneau the next day. It was a town I'd longed to see ever since, as a young teenager, I'd read about it in a schoolgirly book. It had sounded magical. However, Liz and Ian said, "You must go to Pointe du Raz. The boys will love the big waves there." (That's where they had just come from). They also urged us to go to Bénodet, on the south coast of Brittany, because they'd stayed there in a super campsite that had a fabulous swimming pool *and* a jacuzzi.

We got out the map and planned a new route to Pointe du Raz, trusting that the campsite would be as good as this one.

CHAPTER FIVE

The wild West

Pentrez Plage to Pointe du Raz

The next morning Liz and Ian were ready to go before us, but they'd only had bread and jam for their breakfast. We each had a three-egg omelette to give us a good start (as Dervla Murphy might have done, although that was probably all that was available for her). I didn't know how Ian was going to manage with his back, but once on his bike he seemed able to pedal. We arranged to see them both on the 8 am ferry out of Roscoff in just over a week's time.

About midday we set off in brilliant sunshine, leaving the strong sea breeze behind us, and the beautiful beach. It was quite a wrench, but we felt a certain amount of excited anticipation.

There was a lesser breeze now and the boys were cycling topless. From my usual position at the rear I observed that all their teenage spots had cleared up and they had lovely tanned backs.

I was wearing my new visor-cum-headband. It was red with a red Perspex peak. Having a rather small head, I'd had to put a tuck in the elastic with a safety pin, but every time I careered downhill the bloomin' thing blew off. After going back uphill twice to fetch it, I got wise and pulled it down round my neck when we were going fast. Malc called it my 'pelican bib'.

We reached the outskirts of Douarnenez and decided not to plunge down to the town centre. It was such a challenging descent and we'd only just struggled up a long, tiring climb. Quite a shame really, I would like to have seen it from sea level. It was a largish fishing port.

Keeping up on the high road, we soon came upon an enormous hypermarket. We had never seen anything on this scale before. It had roads and underpasses built especially to serve it. Visits to supermarkets were becoming the highlights of our holiday. We knew that whatever troublesome things we had to put up with, we could always buy some tasty, more affordable treats in a supermarket.

This vast place sold everything imaginable and first of all I wanted to look at the prices of pillows and cushions, even a geriatric rubber ring; anything to put under my hips to ensure a comfy night's sleep. It didn't take me long to realise though, that these luxuries were far too expensive and if I bought anything, I would have to carry it. Rather sadly I gave up the idea and headed for the food section.

When we emerged we were carrying loads of cheap green grapes, two litres of orange juice, peaches, crisps, bread, cheese slices, chocolate and other good things to eat. "Enough for a banquet", Tom said. But, as there was nowhere to sit, we ate almost everything standing up in the car park.

Absolutely full to bursting, we continued on our way. Now we had reached the north coast of the peninsula. Pointe du Raz was at the very end of this, about the most westerly point of Brittany. We were feeling on a high – the weather was perfect and the pedalling fairly easy. Far down to our right, when there was a gap in the greenery, we got glimpses of the sparkling sea. It whetted our appetites and spurred us on to our destination, where the big waves would come crashing in.

At about 6.30 pm we descended a very steep hill to a bay next to Pointe du Raz. What a shock! It seemed quite desolate, like being in the middle of Wales. Where was the campsite?

On either side of the bay were high hills, sandy and covered with coarse grass. Two white hotels stood in the valley bottom, looking rather forlorn and lifeless. There were also two kiosks near them. In one was a telephone and the other looked as though it might house a toilet, but it was locked. On the edge of the beach was a tent covering a lifeboat and, not far from it, a snack-caravan that appeared to be closed. That was it. Why had we assumed that Liz and Ian had camped on a proper site? They could have told us. What were we going to eat? All we had was dry Weetabix.

A German couple in a Volkswagen van parked on the hillside, told us they had been camping there for a week and there was a good shop - about ten miles away. "Thanks" we thought. Also there was a tap somewhere up the side of the hill, but we never found it. Apart from them, there was not a soul to be seen.

The boys didn't seem very concerned and began playing boules with the fascinating, big round pebbles that were everywhere. (Part of the beach was cobbled with them). I wandered around near the lifeboat tent and found a tap with a short hose attached. The connection had a lock on it but there was no key.

I chivvied the boys and said we *must* find somewhere to put up the tents, so reluctantly they finished their game, and with enormous effort we heaved our bikes up the sandy track. About halfway to the top, on the side of Pointe du Raz, we found three concrete bunkers from the Second World War, with lots of connecting passages. Pete, Tom and Malc dropped everything and dashed over to explore. Eventually, when they had crawled down every accessible passage, they came back to me, prepared at last, to assist.

On the only flat piece of ground we could find, we managed to erect the tents. There wasn't room to line them up together. In fact, there was barely room to fit them in at all. We left the panniers strapped onto the bikes. There was no point in unpacking.

In the late evening sunshine we observed some movement in the snack caravan and went galloping down the track to see if it was open. It was. We could have something to eat, at last. Apart from Pete, who was still full up from the hypermarket feast, the rest of us were feeling quite peckish. At great expense (on our budget), Tom, Malc and I each had a meagre portion of 'frites'. The couple in the van promised they'd bring us two baguettes in the morning – well it would actually be around midday, they told us. The sun was sinking as we climbed back up the hill to bed.

It was a windy night. If the sea at Pentrez Plage had sounded like roaring engines, here it was like warfare. The waves cracked like cannon-fire on to the rocks. And as if this noise wasn't enough to stop me sleeping, the fact that we were camped so near to the 'gun-lookouts' with all their hidden mysteries gave me the creeps.

But I must have dropped off to sleep, because I awoke to feel Malc shaking me vigorously. He whispered hoarsely into my ear that someone was RIGHT OUTSIDE. Whoever it was, he said, had stopped by the bikes for a while and just now had brushed against the tent. I went cold all over and felt around for the sharp pointed knife I used for cutting bread. I clasped it down by my side. I was rigid with fear. There was no way I would be going back to sleep now.

We held our breath until we were almost bursting, listening intently. After a while, when nothing else happened and there were no more sounds outside, we relaxed a little. Then we were startled again by loud banging sounds. We couldn't make them out. Sometimes they seemed to be coming from the bunkers, at others, they sounded as if people were breaking into the hotels down below. It completely flummoxed us and we were on 'high alert' for the rest of the night.

* * * * *

Malc and I were convinced we'd see some sort of destruction

The boys begin playing boules at Pointe du Raz

We pitched our tents on a ledge overlooking La Baie des Trépassés

Pete on La Baie des Trépassés with his 'sail bike'

Pointe du Raz - the calm side

to the hotels – broken doors or windows, perhaps? But when we unzipped our tent and looked out, everything seemed to be as it should be. The hotels looked intact and as lifeless as ever. What *had* been going on in the night? We were baffled. Pete and Tom hadn't heard a thing! But we hadn't imagined it.

Next we checked our bikes and belongings. Nothing appeared to be missing. Then we noticed that our tents were pitched right on a pathway from the hotels to the top of the hill, where a couple of houses stood on the brow.

It suddenly dawned on us that we must be pitched on the 'flight path' from what we'd thought were redundant hotels. A late night reveller, coming uphill in the dark, had probably had as much of a shock as us when he'd tripped on our bikes and stumbled by our tents. Phew, so much for our close encounter with death!

We all felt somewhat washed out that morning in spite of the beautiful sunshine and the panoramic view from our vantage point over the Baie des Trépassés. Our mouths were as dry as could be. We had drunk the last dregs of our water the previous evening and hadn't thought to ask for a refill at the snack-caravan. There was nothing to eat either, apart from wretched dry Weetabix of course. But we were far too thirsty for those. We'd have to hang around until midday for the snack-caravan to open. The baguettes we'd ordered didn't seem very appetising right now.

After a while, though, we rallied round and decided to do *something* with this sunny morning. Pete took the opportunity to make a wind sail from the extended flysheet, which we hadn't used the night before to join the tents together. He rigged up a contraption with poles and string and attached it to his handlebars like a sail. Then he and Tom went down to the beach to try it out. I followed with my camera.

There was only a light breeze blowing, otherwise Pete's sail-bike would surely have zipped along the beach, just like the land yachts we'd seen. Such a shame! At least it absorbed the two boys for ages.

Malc came down to draw pictures in the damp sand. He'd been very influenced by Tom's beach drawings at Pentrez Plage. Tom was superb at cartoon drawing.

The Baie was filling up with weekend visitors now. We saw quite a few British cars parking on the beach and what to me looked like a football team getting off a coach. This team was led all around the cliff paths for a long jog. I followed their progress up and down distant pathways. Once back on the beach, they were put through a series of exercises that made them look quite stupid. I laughed inwardly. Having instructed exercise classes myself, I conceitedly thought that I could have made a much better job of it.

We kept watching the snack caravan to see if the owners had arrived yet. Each time a car came into the parking area we thought, "It *must* be them this time." But it never was.

I went for a paddle in the sea. The waves were no bigger here than those at Pentrez Plage. (It was on the other side of Pointe du Raz that the great Atlantic rollers came crashing in. We could certainly hear them from this side).

72

Although the bay was quite wide, there was only a narrow strip of beach between two flags where bathing was allowed. The lifeboat was standing ready for action, with a couple of young, tanned lifeguards on watch.

Taking the camera, I walked down by the hotels to cross the bay, giving my prettiest smile to the dishy lifeguards as I passed by them.

I wanted to get a photo of our campsite from the other side. While I was over there, I heard the curious loud banging sounds again. More like booms than bangs. A few seconds later, the sounds echoed on the other side of the bay. So was it perhaps something to do with mining? Nothing at all to do with break-ins at the hotels nor even riots in the gun-lookouts; and Malc and I had stayed on red alert all night!

As I walked back, I could make out the tiny figures of Malc and Tom walking up the cliff path towards the end of Pointe du Raz, recognising them only by the colour of their clothes. I wished I'd been with them. Neither Pete nor I saw the other side of the peninsular with the waves pounding onto the rocks. Later on, I found that they'd almost been cut off by the tide and also, in places, the path was dangerously close to the edge. It's far less traumatic to learn these facts later!

When I arrived at our tents, Pete was sitting there looking miserable, probably wishing he'd eaten a portion of chips the previous night. It was past midday, so I started to gather my belongings together. Malc and Tom returned and we began taking the tents down in silence.

Finally, we saw signs of life in the snack-caravan. Tom

immediately said he was going down to get a drink. My hackles rose. I wasn't letting him skive off now, when we'd almost finished packing up. I told him he could jolly well stay to help us, then we could all go down together, taking everything with us. He didn't argue. Perhaps he just hadn't thought it through.

Soon the bikes were loaded up. We slipped and skidded them down the steep, sandy path to the beach, eager for sustenance from the snack-caravan. I asked the couple there if they would kindly fill our water bottles, but they refused. There was a tap behind the lifeboat tent, they told us. (Well, we already knew that.) All the same I went over to it and found that, praise be, there was now a key to unlock it – and all this time our tongues had been sticking to the roofs of our mouths.

We filled our bottles, gulping and guzzling them empty again, then went back to the caravan for our baguettes. But I was too mean to buy anything to put inside them, at their prices. However, I did go as far as buying a portion of expensive chips for each of us, plus a large packet of the chocolate-filled biscuits. They weren't half as nice as depicted on the packet, but we needed to fill up on carbohydrates. The cost of fruit drinks here was extortionate. For the price of one glassful we could buy two litres of fruit juice in a supermarket. So we filled up the water bottles again.

Sitting at a picnic table to chill out, it took us nearly an hour to feel ready for cycling. Now, with a bit more enthusiasm, we set off up a seemingly endless hill out of the bay, on the opposite side to the one we'd come in on. It was really hot and hard work but once at the top, the road levelled out. Now we were heading slightly south of eastwards, along the bottom of the peninsula.

At Audierne we crossed an estuary and continued on to Plouhinec. Here we followed the gently undulating coastal road south for several miles. It was easy, relaxing cycling; just right for the way we were feeling. Down this coast all the houses had low roofs and were painted white. They looked pleasant, but the scenery was not spectacular. When we were close to the shore we could see outcrops of black rocks, just visible above the water. There were sure to be other rocks hidden treacherously below the surface. No good for swimming.

In one village, we passed a lady who was struggling to get into the driving seat of her little Renault car. She was wearing a very tall, white-laced Breton hat and in order to get in, she had to push it right back horizontally, so that it was lying along the inside of the car roof. It looked hilarious, and we laughed our heads off.

Now and again we came across caravans and camper-vans parked up in quiet locations on grass verges. Like them, we could have camped at any of these places, but with no water supply or shop at hand, it was a bit pointless for us. We'd been there! So we kept going until, to our surprise, the road fizzled out in front of a smart café-cum-restaurant. We asked a girl behind the counter if there were any campsites in the area. She pointed across the fields and we could just see the top of a tent above a hedge. That was a bit of good luck.

The campsite seemed so near, yet we couldn't find how

to get to it. We bumped along a winding track until we came to a huge, stinking pond. It was completely covered in revolting green vegetation, and smelled foul. The boys found some hefty stones and hoicked them into the water. Each big plop spewed up thick black gunge. But then they heard moorhens in the reeds and stopped throwing, incredulous to think that *any* creature could possibly live in such a disgusting environment.

The lane continued meandering. We were shaken to bits by its stones and covered in its dust. Eventually we reached an old farmhouse with the fields on every side designated to camping. There was no sign of any farming. As we gently lowered our bikes to the ground, a woman appeared from the next field and told us we *must* go and announce our arrival immediately.

The farm couple were a lovely old pair, walking around the yard in clogs, wearing old slippers inside them. The two of them tried as hard as us to make conversation. The wife had a high-pitched giggle and wore a headscarf knotted at the front, like a charwoman. She reminded me of Hilda Ogden from Coronation Street. Her husband could speak a bit of German, so if we couldn't understand each other in French, we had a bit more mileage with a smattering of German.

There was no form-filling or paper-signing. He just took us round to a small field on the other side of the farm, making us feel like newly-found relatives. The plot looked more like a sheltered garden than a camping pitch. It had high hedges on three sides, and ruins of an old building on the other. We had it all to ourselves. Vigorous brambles sprouted out all over the wall, so we had to be very careful how we propped our bikes against it.

As it was only about teatime and still hot, I thought the boys might like to go into the sea first. We could put the tents up later. We'd already looked at the beach; the tide was in and it appeared to be pretty well rock-free.

I didn't go with them. A carton of powdered milk had burst inside my panniers and made a real mess over everything. It needed my urgent attention. But even before I'd finished sorting it out, Malc appeared back at my side. He told me, emphatically, that he wasn't going in the sea *any* more. Apparently, while he was paddling, he'd walked into some hidden rocks. Then a wave had knocked him over into a big hole. He looked quite shaken and hung around with me, quiet as a lamb.

When Pete and Tom returned, happy and contented, we put up the tents quicker than we'd ever done before. The ground was just right for camping and the pegs went in a treat.

I set off to find a shop I'd been told about. It was a mile or so inland, in the next village. Inside, the shop was dark and old-fashioned and I was served by an equally old-fashioned but friendly old lady, wearing little round glasses and with her hair in a bun. As we'd used up all the cooking oil and sugar, these would need replacing. I bought all the essentials first, including a rather nice semi-brown loaf. (It turned out to be really tasty). The milk was in a very flimsy plastic bottle with a pointed top which had to be clipped off. Then I bought a tiny packet of raisins to have with our Weetabix in the morning, and tomato sauce, biscuits and cider for extra treats. I'd overspent my allowance for the day. Tomorrow, I decided, we ought to fill up on potatoes.

The water tap was right round on the other side of the farm. It stuck out of the wall above an ancient stone trough, which seemed old enough to be Roman, I thought. The buildings next to it held two toilets and a shower. They stood in a row, looking more like old cowsheds than anything else. The toilets were a hoot – real Heath Robinson contrivances. In the bottom of each toilet pan was a rusty tin tray and by the side of each toilet, a flimsy wire extended from the roof down into the floor. At seat level there was a handle attached which bore some resemblance to a wire coat hanger. When this was pulled, the tin tray tipped up and a feeble trickle of water washed down the pan. It was an ingenious DIY job. "Not very good for big jobs" I heard Tom proclaim, but it was in keeping with the rest of the place. It didn't seem to put people off staying; there were plenty of campers here.

My bed that night was the comfiest ever. I snuggled into my sleeping bag, looking forward to a night of blissful slumber, especially after the two beakers of cider I'd consumed. Then, unbelievably, my other big toe began hurting and it kept me awake for hours on end. Those bloody cheap plimsolls! The cider turned out to be only apple juice, so that didn't aid my sleep at all, although I didn't realise this at the time. It had cost more than the cider too!

CHAPTER SIX

Exploring southern Brittany

Penhors and Bénodet

By the time the boys were awake it was becoming hot inside the tents. Intense rays of sunlight bore down through the two layers of our cheap little shelters. Today was going to be a scorcher. When we crawled out into our living area we were horrified to find flies - EVERYWHERE. They were massed, wing-tip to wing-tip, over every square inch of the flysheet (was this why it was called a flysheet?)

They weren't huge, but they seemed as ghastly as a plague of locusts. We hastily zipped up the tents to keep them out of our sleeping quarters. Watching them crawl over everything, our beakers and plates, cutlery and kettle, pans and panniers, we were mortified. I quickly rescued the Weetabix before they got inside the box and the bottle of milk. Then I asked one of the boys to fetch a bowl of water so that I could wash the utensils we'd need for breakfast. This we ate at the bottom of our garden to escape the worst of the infestation. Here at least, in the shade of the hedge, we found a little respite. I'd never experienced anything like those flies or that heat.

We thought we should stay out of the tents all day, but we propped the flysheet open, hoping the flies would leave when they'd had enough. Pete and Tom, undeterred by the heatwave, planned to surf in the sea again. They told Malc there was a long expanse of sandy beach further down to the south, no rocks at all, and it was just unfortunate that he'd chosen a rocky bit to paddle in yesterday.

They set off, taking the short-cut path to the beach. A little later Malc followed, "just to walk about", he told me. I said I'd join them later, when I'd cleared up.

I filled our water bottles and put them into my haversack together with a large packet of biscuits. Then, giving the flies a withering scowl and a curse, I set off to find the boys. Four bottles of water felt really heavy to carry, especially with another painful toenail to cope with. I took off my shoes and carried those as well.

For ages I walked southwards down the sandy beach looking for the boys, with the straps of that dratted haversack digging into my shoulders. The three of them were nowhere to be seen. I turned round and came all the way back. When I reached my starting point I saw Malc hanging about aimlessly. He hadn't seen any sign of Pete or Tom. I eased the haversack off my sore shoulders and we drank most of our water and ate half the biscuits, just to make the bag lighter. Then we set off down the beach to do another recce, with Malc now carrying the haversack for me.

This time we trudged even further south. Still there was no sign of Pete or Tom. We felt really fed up as we plodded slowly back on the hot sand. It was as if we were crossing a desert, though not a deserted one, for the beach was filling up with Sunday visitors. We had to keep walking round their towels and windbreaks. They were all having so much fun. We weren't. We felt as if we were doing penance.

Arriving back to where we'd started from yet again, we happened to glance northwards up the beach to where the rocks jutted out – and there, just a stone's throw away, were the other two boys having the time of their lives. Malc and I seethed. Our whole morning had been spent under sufferance. Oh well, I thought, at least my lobster-red legs had now turned to a lovely rosy brown.

The tide was out, leaving the rocks exposed on the beach, so there was no danger of being washed on to them by the waves. Hordes of people were in the sea now. I felt a great urge to do likewise, but I'd left my swimming costume and towel in the tent. I wasn't going to walk all the way back for those. So I waded in, in my shorts.

Before the holiday, I had made these shorts from blue towelling material. I'd even dyed some of it a lovely shade of purple to sew around the curved, bottom edge as a border. This design of shorts was very popular (although not in towelling material) but I hadn't been able to find any in the charity shops. Hence, the great lengths I'd gone to to create my own. They weren't comfy enough to cycle in, with their lumpy seams, but now they could double-up as bikini bottoms.

It was absolutely glorious in the water. The only way to bear the heat was to be wet. Even Malc came in to join us, although he didn't have his surfboard. Pete and Tom let us take turns on theirs. When it was my turn, they tried their hardest to capsize me on every big wave, but whatever trick they tried, they couldn't tip me off. I was invincible. We had such a laugh, enhanced by watching the stupidity of older people. The antics they got up to! I suppose they were just trying to recreate their youth. (Rather like me, really.)

As time went by I was aware that my shorts were getting longer and longer, until they were nearly down to my knees and the elastic round the waist was struggling to keep them up. They looked like some enormous nappy. How on earth was I going to walk back up the beach in these? We'd spent all this time laughing at other people, now they'd *all* be laughing at me.

Eventually I had to get out of the sea. The boys had had enough and were starving. So, keeping as close behind them as I could, I self-consciously followed them out of the water. With my eyes fixed to the ground I shuffled up the beach, hanging onto the waistband to stop the shorts from falling off. It seemed to take forever to reach the hedges of our short-cut lane, where I could escape from view. Of course I hadn't heard a single laugh or titter. In fact I don't think I had been noticed at all, not me or my 'hanging bags'. I was such a silly worrier.

The good news was that there were far fewer flies in the tent. The bad news was that when Malc and Tom went off on their bikes with a shopping list, they came back empty-handed. The shop was closed on Sundays. Oh dear, what could I cook for tea? We had eight eggs and the Weetabix. It would have to be potatoes, after all.

After changing out of my enormous shorts I went to the farmhouse to see if they could sell me any. Hilda Ogden took me into a barn and, giggling and chirping all the while, weighed me a generous bagfull for only 3F.

There was the arduous task of boiling the kettle to wash the plates and cutlery again before we could even think of eating. The boys were ravenous. So, while I was peeling and cutting all the spuds, I let them go to the posh café to buy cornettos out of today's food money; almost 10F each.

I made loads of chips, frying one person's portion at a time, together with two eggs each. The first lot of chips were a bit soggy, but each batch improved. It took ages and ages. Malc went to bed while I was still cooking, it went on for so long! By the time I got to eat mine, I was worn out and the sun had set.

I'd used half the new cooking oil and didn't know whether to save it or not. So I left it in the saucepan next to the tent, with a lid loosely over it. There were lots of greasy plates and utensils to wash, but that was the last thing I felt like doing now. I submerged them all in a bowl of cold water and went to bed.

* * * * *

Long before dawn, Malc and I became aware of an intermittent flashing light. There must be a lighthouse nearby. But then the telltale rumbles started and we braced ourselves for a thunderstorm.

I'd been dreading a storm at night. We seemed so vulnerable in our little tents. In fact, the reality wasn't half so scary as we'd imagined, because this storm wasn't a patch on the one we'd cycled through just over a week before. The rain was torrential for a while but then it stopped suddenly, leaving just thunder and lightning which went on for a very long time indeed. Now *that* was worrying for me, because someone had told me that it's better to have rain with lightning, to help earth the electricity. So when the whole lot eventually rumbled away, I breathed a big sigh of relief.

Tom slept through it all. When it was light, three of us got up, leaving him to his slumbers. It was a beautiful bright day but not blazing hot like the previous day. After Pete had cycled over to the shop to fetch us bread and milk we ate our last share of Weetabix. The flies had nearly all departed, thank goodness.

When Tom had woken up and eaten his breakfast, we began the task of packing up. Rainwater had got into the chip oil I'd left in the saucepan, so I chucked it into a patch of tall nettles. I still had half a bottle. When I transferred this into my ex-shampoo bottle, it filled it right to the brim. Now I had to get stuck into the greasy washing up from the night before. What a fag!

I set a kettleful of water on the stove to boil. Pete and Malc started taking the tents down while Tom packed up his own stuff and strapped it on to his bike. He was about to wander off to fill his water bottles when I called him back (in rather strong language), telling him to bloody well help with the tents, then we could *all* go and fill our water bottles. It was the washing up that was annoying me really.

I went to pay Hilda Ogden. The charge was very reasonable – only 40F for two nights or the equivalent of £4. (Not many mod cons, though!) There was more giggling as she and I tried to make conversation at the back door. Her distinctive voice could be heard throughout the day as she chatted to the campers. She seemed to know them all, so I supposed they were regular visitors.

We filled our bottles at the water hole and I hurriedly pumped up my tyres, not wanting to hold the boys up any longer. But as I screwed up the valve nozzle on the back wheel, it turned round and round and wouldn't tighten. In my haste, I chose to ignore it.

I raced to catch up with the boys, who were already rolling nicely along the road, looking forward to finding the plush campsite in Bénodet. However, before I was even through the farm gate, my tyre had gone absolutely flat. I called the boys back. They returned reluctantly, looking irritated.

As quickly as possible I took off my panniers, so that Pete could take the wheel out. Luckily, we'd brought a spare tube from England to fit the 26" wheels on my bike and Malc's. Soon the job was done. I should have realised that the valve had broken. What an idiot I was. Served me right for swearing at Tom, I thought. Not that *I* was paying the penalty; it was Pete who had changed the inner tube for me.

For some reason, Malc was bursting with energy and was charging ahead of us all. For another reason, probably too much heat yesterday, Pete was feeling under the weather and stayed at the back. He was also fed up with acting as a windbreak for the rest of us - it was windy.

The first town we came to, only seven miles up the road, was Ploneour Lanvern on the D2. On the other side of it we found a Rallye Supermarché and stopped to buy some treats. The cheap camping had given a boost to our food allowance.

This time we bought eight Mars Bar ice-creams in a pack, lots of fruit, the usual two litres of fruit juice and a pack of sliced 'Texas beef'. (All the sliced meat in packs tasted like bacon, whether it was ham, pork or Texas beef!) We bought many more things, including oil for the bikes. The chains had gone dry and rusty since our deluge day. Our coffee had also run out, but instead of replacing it, I bought a large plastic jar of chocolate drink called 'Benco'. When we came outside, Malc told me he didn't like chocolate drinks. I was quite cross with him, because he'd watched me buying this huge jar and hadn't said a word.

We stood under an awning outside the shop and ate all our goodies. It was drizzling a little now, but it didn't dampen our spirits and soon stopped. After we'd oiled the chains we continued on our way.

The food money I'd had in cash had all been spent now. I would need to change some traveller's cheques. In the next town, Pont l'Abbé, we went to look for a bank. Unfortunately they were all closed on Mondays. I asked Pete and Malc if they would lend me some of their spending money. They had worked hard to earn it – Pete doing his evening paper-round and Malc washing the baker's van on Saturday mornings, plus filling in on the paper-round now and then. Grandma had also given them some money, which they'd very gratefully accepted. Even so, their overall amount was quite modest, but they didn't hesitate to help out.

I had estimated, rather optimistically, that our camping and food costs would be about £20 per day. Tom's dad had paid a quarter share of this. However, in spite of some of our cheaper overnights, we were now reduced to rather less than this amount. But we still needed treats to boost our morale from time to time, and these times were becoming more frequent.

We were cycling along the D44, which we knew was close to a large sea inlet, but we couldn't see it. In my heart I was feeling rather disappointed. I could sense that this area wouldn't be as exciting as we'd expected. There was also more traffic about than we'd become accustomed to, but we were lucky enough to be in a cycle lane. We sped along the fairly flat road, racing for several miles with our pedals spinning fast.

As we came near to Bénodet there was a wonderful bridge called the Pont-de-Cornouaille, spanning the estuary of the river Odet. The cycle lane did weird and wonderful things around the roundabouts and when we approached the bridge, the track led us into a large layby. The cars continued straight on and were caught in a toll-trap, while we whizzed round the layby and back on to the road that led to the bridge. This was now fairly narrow, with no cycle lane at all. We found it hard not to wobble as we struggled up the incline with our heavy loads. If we lost momentum we might fall off, putting ourselves at the mercy of the traffic.

On reaching the top we found a viewing point, where spectators could admire the panorama. Puffing and panting, we took advantage of this to get our breath back and enjoy the view from both sides.

From now on it was mainly downhill to Bénodet. The boys were searching for 'Eldorado'. Well, not quite. Just a campsite with a jacuzzi and swimming pool. As it happened, though, we didn't do any searching and rode straight into the first site that we came to, deciding to stay there. It was the nearest to town and was beautifully laid out. There was no swimming pool and no jacuzzi, but suddenly no one cared. We couldn't be bothered. Our spirits had lost a bit of impetus!

The site was divided into pretty plots, each surrounded by young hedges and trees. We went almost to the top of the site and put up our tents under a hedge of oak trees that formed the boundary. On the other side of this hedge, the ground dropped down into grassy fields.

At the top of the site was a caravan with two tents pitched alongside it. In front of these was a large table around which several young men sat eating. They were very noisy. A tall, rather smart tent was pitched below us, occupied by four French girls. They too, were quite noisy.

I suspect we were all disappointed with Bénodet. As we'd ridden along by the beach we'd noticed that the sea was as gentle as a millpond. Where were all these big waves we'd been expecting on the south coast? Such a shame! Maybe we shouldn't have come here at all. *My* desire, of course, was to go to Concarneau (only twelve miles away). However, I just wanted the boys to have a good time. What a pity Liz and Ian had filled us with these great expectations. I still hoped, secretly, that perhaps I'd get to see Concarneau. Maybe one of the boys would come with me.

Nevertheless, the campsite was extremely pleasant. Sitting in our plot was like sitting in our own pretty garden. There was a shop on the site, which sold a good variety of things. I treated us to some margarine, as a change from eating dry bread. (It wasn't something you could carry around in hot weather.) For tea that night we had omelette and beans with a big bag of crisps. I didn't much like the French version of baked beans. Malc disliked them even more, but when you're hungry you just have to eat something. As we would now have to manage on about £15 a day for everything, beans might feature fairly regularly.

That evening the girls seemed to be in high spirits. They were Ooh-la-la-ing the boys, who were extremely flattered and kept racing up and down the site on their bikes, passing close by them.

It was a fairly uneventful night, except that acorns kept dropping on to the tent at very irregular intervals, making us jump. In the early hours of the morning there was a great deal of clattering and banging in the top plot. We assumed the young men were doing a moonlight flit.

* * * * *

In fact the caravan and tents were still there in the morning and everything was very quiet until midday. It was the sort of day when you expect the sun to come out at any moment and make all the misty cloud go away, but this didn't happen until about 2.30pm. Even then, the sunshine only lasted for half an hour. By that time, boredom and lethargy had set in and the boys didn't want to go anywhere or do anything.

That morning I had my first hot water shower of the holiday. It was bliss. I savoured it for far too long and before I knew it, there was a 'click' and the water ran cold. I hadn't even rinsed the shampoo out of my hair.

Afterwards, I cycled into town to look for a bank. I scoured the main street; it was the only street. When I could find no bank at all, I began to feel rather disconcerted. I had to change some travellers' cheques pretty soon. Then I noticed several people going into an office. Through the glass door I could see a long queue. Outside, a small sign implied that this was, indeed, a money exchange office. I locked up my bike and marched to the door. There was no handle, so I tried to push it open – but it was locked, so all that happened was that I hit my head on the glass.

I stood outside, bewildered and embarrassed after my bold approach. Several faces in the queue turned to look at me. I blushed. No one came to open the door, so I rapped on the glass. A second later the door swung open, all by itself.

One man was running the office alone, well enclosed

behind safety glass. He was controlling the door with a button on his desk. There were about 20 people in front of me in the queue, all English and all smart. I felt a right country bumpkin in my creased, rolled-up shorts and rather hairy legs! My hair was a mess too; all fly-away and out of control.

The next couple who entered weren't so smart and I felt more comfortable with them. We got chatting. They told me they were camping on the other side of Bénodet and were going on coach tours most days. I discovered that Quimper, the nearest city, was pronounced 'Kampair'. In fact, when we saw a sign the next day, the Breton spelling was 'Kamper'.

I did a little shopping. This was such a touristy place that there were no bargains to be had anywhere. All I took back was bread, milk and a few plums.

Exchanging my travellers' cheques had taken absolutely ages and it was now almost lunchtime. I didn't know that Malc had been looking for me most of the morning, but we'd missed each other. He'd walked into town because the gear cable on his bike had broken. While we were at Pentrez Plage, the cable had begun to split and one or two strands had broken. We did have a spare one but we'd just kept forgetting to replace it.

That morning, to Malc's great annoyance, Pete had been racing around the campsite on Malc's bike. It was then that the gear cable had finally snapped. So I'd told Pete that *he* must put the new one on. However, when I arrived back, the job was still waiting to be done. Pete and Tom were sitting about aimlessly. Pete, who, up until now had been so dependable whenever anything needed mending or adjusting, decided that he was not going to do this job for Malc. There was a slight problem though; the new cable had a hammer shape on one end and a pear shape on the other. Depending on which shape fitted your mechanism, the other end had to be cut off. Our pliers had proved to be inadequate for the job.

Determined that Pete must mend Malc's gears, I strode off to the camp office. Hopefully, the man in there would have a tool sharp enough to clip the end off the cable. 'La femme' was in the office. She picked up a bunch of keys and took me to the men's toilets. Feeling uncomfortable, I hung around outside while she unlocked a door somewhere within. I could hear her clattering about. Eventually, I ventured in. It seemed to be safe. Together, we tried pliers, cutters, pincers – everything. What blunt tools and what a tough cable! At last, we managed to chew through the blessed thing and cut the hammer end off. I thanked her and took the mangled, splay-ended cable back to Pete.

Reluctantly he started to do the job, but reckoned that the cable-end was far too frayed to go through the tiny hole on the frame. I was cross and told him he'd *got* to do it. But in the end he flung the whole lot down on the grass and stormed off on his bike. Trying hard not to become too ruffled, I began making Texas beef sandwiches.

Next thing I knew, lazy Tom was patiently having a go. Before long, he'd managed to get the cable through the hole. But poor lad, he realised he'd put it in on the wrong side of the chain, so now he had to pull it out and do it all over again.

He worked quietly, with no fuss at all. In my eyes, I felt he'd redeemed himself considerably. I had a new respect for him.

Malc was delighted, when he eventually came back from looking for me. He tried out his bike and found that the gears changed like a dream. Pete was somewhat put out, even a little amazed, that Tom had done the job. After lunch, Malc rode off on his bike, while Pete and Tom hung around again listlessly.

There seemed to be only one young man left in the plot at the top. He was seated at a table with a guitar on his knee. On it, he plonked out discordant chords to accompany the English records he was playing, extremely loudly, on a turntable. To us, they seemed an appalling choice of records, made worse by his contributions. I couldn't make out if he was a *jazz* guitarist or a *bad* guitarist! We were somewhat amused by him though, and he obviously enjoyed an audience. The girls were very quiet today – maybe they had hangovers!

It looked as if the sun had come out to stay. I put on my bikini top to get a tan. But I was wasting my time, for quite soon the sun disappeared again and I was searching for warmer clothes to put on. What a boring day! If only I could interest the boys in surfing in the sea.

I studied the map. To the east, there was a long spit of sand which looked to be at right angles to the Atlantic current. Surely we would find some big waves there, once we got away from the wide estuary of the river Odet. However, this sand spit, although tantalisingly close to Bénodet, was not quite connected to the mainland, being cut off by a channel of water. The only way to reach it was by going right to the other end, near Pointe de Mousterlin, several miles eastwards.

The two boys weren't particularly interested in my findings. Feeling peeved, I thought, "blow you, I'll go on my own, then." I wasn't really happy about cycling off by myself to anywhere which was as yet unknown. We had no way of getting in touch if anything untoward happened to any of us. (If the world had been full of people like me, the Americas would still be undiscovered and kings and knights would not have gone on crusades.) But me, being me, I felt rather brave setting off on my quest.

After following the Fouesnant road for a while, I saw a sign pointing left for Pointe de Mousterlin. However, seeing no more signposts after that, I arrived at a dead end somewhere behind the sand spit, in front of a huge dyke. People in long boots were wading about in thick mud, wielding their fishing nets. I was still quite near the estuary.

I asked a couple in a car parked nearby if they could give me directions. They went to great lengths to explain the way, making sure I understood. It was complicated and I thanked them for their time. But not being confident that I could remember correctly, I re-checked with a man who was standing at a junction, only a short distance away. He instructed me using vigorous arm gestures and I felt quite embarrassed when the couple I'd just consulted drove by and saw me asking all over again.

After following a contorted route for some time, hoping I'd

got my directions correct, I emerged from a single-track lane onto a main road. That didn't seem right, so I back-tracked up this lane until I came to a farmhouse with a 'Cidre' sign outside. A German couple came to the door. In broken English they told me the way. The man also added, in semi-sign language, that it was a nudist beach – well – fifty/fifty! Did he mean half-naked or half the people? Surely the boys would be interested in swimming here now, if only I could find the place!

It seemed a long way. But at last I found it. On either side of Pointe de Mousterlin were enormous expanses of steeply-sloping beaches, with boats pulled up on to the sandbanks as far as the eye could see. To the east, I could faintly make out Beg-Meil in the misty distance. Just think; Concarneau was only a few miles beyond that. Maybe I saw a few naked bodies, but they were too far away for me to be sure.

Anyway, I had to get back and try to muster up some enthusiasm. I realised, too late, that I'd forgotten to notice if there were any big waves. I'd been daydreaming about Concarneau again.

I took a different route back; it was much too complicated to remember the way I'd come. So I kept to the main road, overtaking French cyclists on the way. They were all over the road as usual, in fact, four abreast! No wonder French drivers give cyclists such a wide berth.

When I came to a main junction it was left for Bénodet, and right for Concarneau. So near yet so far! But I had to get back to the boys.

Fouesnant was straight across this junction. I thought I

95

might as well have a quick peep, to see what this town was like. En route I noted a small supermarket where I could stock up with provisions on my way back.

At a café-cum-bed-and-breakfast establishment I stopped to glance at postcards on a rack outside. A nauseating smell, a mixture of pungent food and strong disinfectant, wafted through the door. Covering my nose with one hand, I carried on looking, hoping there might be a postcard of Concarneau. A couple arrived by bike and on seeing the B&B sign, decided they'd stay there. Yuk! How could anyone put up with that pong?

Eavesdropping on their conversation, I discovered that they'd just cycled from Pentrez Plage. That's what we could have done. Instead, I'd allowed my plans to be altered by Liz and Ian's suggestions (to head for Pointe du Raz where we'd ended up in the middle of nowhere). However, as I surveyed my surroundings, I realised that this area didn't inspire me very much at all. It was rather flat and featureless. Also there were too many tourists. After all my wistful thinking, perhaps Concarneau wouldn't live up to my expectations either. Reflecting a while, I decided that I was glad we'd taken the wild and rugged route.

The thought entered my mind that if I didn't get back soon the boys would be worrying about me. Or was that wishful thinking? Inside the poky supermarket I stocked up on food bargains and bought a new gas canister. All that chip cooking had used up loads of gas. I was grateful to have Tom's cooker as a supplement.

What a challenge, to organise and pack all my purchases

into the panniers! It took me ages, unpacking and re-packing several times, having bought more than I could really carry. I felt smugly pleased with myself for coping.

Back at the junction, I took one last ponderous look at the Concarneau sign, then headed back to Bénodet.

I told the boys about the beaches, but they were more interested in what I'd bought to eat than where I'd been, or that I was safely 'home'. As it was now getting on for 6 pm, I dutifully got on with making tea. It wasn't exactly hard work, being mainly tinned food; ravioli, plus a few treats.

Malc retired to bed early to do some artwork. Drawing cartoons and graffiti on the camping mats and surfboards had evolved into a major pastime – probably through boredom! But as it was now such a pleasant evening, Pete, Tom and I decided to go for a ride in the dusk.

We followed the coastline eastwards, taking a winding track through a pine forest. The smell of the trees was heavenly in the evening air. We emerged on to a sandy bank leading down to a channel of water. Lo and behold, this was the cut-off end of the sand spit! Tom told me he'd ridden here during the afternoon. The tide had been out and it was possible for him to wade across to the sand-spit with the water barely above his knees. What a wasted afternoon *I'd* had. We could all have come here. Never mind.

Later, back in the tent, Malc told me he wanted to look for some French 'bangers' in the morning, if that was ok by me. I'd heard about these small fireworks before, from a friend of Pete's who'd been on a French exchange holiday. I had slight misgivings but thought they couldn't be very harmful if they were readily available in the French shops. So I said I'd let him buy a few, hoping it might make up for the lack of excitement here.

The return to Roscoff

Bénodet to Châtaulin

Sadly, there were only three days left until the end of our holiday and the time had come to start heading back to Roscoff. I hadn't yet reserved the return tickets. We had 'open' tickets, so our return journey needn't be booked until the day before we planned to leave. These open tickets allowed us to stay for up to five weeks. It would be great to stay longer, but our money was running out. Anyway, we'd arranged to meet Liz and Ian on the ferry.

Three days was ample time for cycling to Roscoff, but just in case anything should go wrong, there would be plenty of time in hand. With effort, we could get there in one day (with an early start and keeping up a good pace). What usually happened, though, was that by the time we'd eaten breakfast, cleared away and taken down the tents, it was almost time for lunch. But today there was no rush. Châtaulin, our intended overnight stop, was only 30 miles away.

When Malc returned from town with his bangers, the three boys slipped stealthily through a gap in the hedge and down into the adjacent field. There, like gunpowder plotters, they embarked on their covert mission. Loud bangs were soon ringing out from behind the oak hedge, resounding all through the campsite. I carried on with my chores regardless, pretending I hadn't heard a thing. But the boys couldn't maintain their secrecy for long. Soon they were whooping with delight. Luckily, no one was about who might be annoyed by them.

It wasn't long before they'd exploded every single banger. They reappeared on the campsite, all fired up and wanting more. Tom and Malc jumped on their bikes and raced into town to stock up again. Pete had reservations and decided not to spend the rest of his money in such a frivolous fashion.

I surveyed the washing-up from the night before. What bad habits I had got into. It's lucky we hadn't become rat infested. Liz and Ian had found a hedgehog inside their tent. Who knows what had been in ours?

Typically, because we were moving on, the weather had brightened up again. Still, it was much nicer to be cycling in sunshine than in cloud or rain. We ought to have felt downhearted knowing that we'd reached the furthest extent of our holiday. Hereafter we'd be heading for home. However, for us, leaving Bénodet wasn't a wrench. We'd found it a bit boring.

We were almost at Quimper when we came across an immense hypermarket, even bigger than the one near Douarnenez. There were roads and underpasses leading to numerous car parks. We were drawn in like magnets. Time for a picnic!

I couldn't help being extravagant, in spite of my financial restraints. We were on holiday, after all. My shopping basket was weighed down with all our goodies, which included four amazingly thick, succulent slices of cooked pork with stuffing. They alone cost the equivalent of £2.30. We took our picnic over to a sunny spot between the trees. There we sat on the lush grass to devour our sumptuous food. The sun's rays bore down on the backs of our necks as we leaned forward to munch through our crusty, pork-filled baguettes. We probably consumed more meat in that meal than we'd eaten all the rest of the holiday.

Quimper was a busy city and therefore more difficult to get through. Nevertheless, it had a pleasant charm about it. The river Odet ran through the middle. It was wide and clear with prestigious-looking old buildings set back on both sides. Dominating the centre was a huge cathedral. I was disappointed that we didn't stop, as I fancied having a better look at the architecture. However, we were all following Pete, not wanting to lose sight of him, or get mown down by the traffic.

All three boys seemed intent on getting through the city centre as quickly as possible. So, when we discovered we'd taken the wrong road and were heading for Rennes, I wasn't disappointed. It meant we had to turn round and come all the way back in.

It took absolutely ages for us to cross the road, and cycling back into the centre on our laden bikes was quite dodgy, with so many parked cars squeezing us out into the traffic. For me, at least, it was worthwhile. Now I could admire the city centre for a short time, while the boys looked for the correct direction to take.

Heading out towards Brest, there was an endless drag of a hill to climb. Having dismounted in the middle of Quimper, we continued pushing the bikes arduously uphill. As we passed tiered, stone-built terraced houses, I was reminded of a typical street in Bath, although the colour of the stone was less mellow here.

From studying the map, we knew that after a few miles there would be a right-hand turn for Châtaulin. But, surprise surprise, our road was suddenly chopped in half by a huge embankment. For the second time on our holiday, some inconsiderate so-and-sos had built a motorway right across our chosen route, bringing us to an abrupt stop.

Now we had to search for an alternative way. We'd had it all so beautifully planned. As the countryside was becoming hillier, we didn't want any lengthy detours. Turning back the way we'd come, we found an insignificant-looking road going in a similar direction. We couldn't see it on our map, so we hoped it would take us to the right place. There was no option but to try it.

At times, the sun was intense. Soon we'd drunk all our water and were absolutely parched. Pedalling along this desolate, narrow road, mile after mile, we wondered how long we could keep going before we died of thirst.

Malc started grumbling about his aching back, and we

were all becoming a bit grumpy. Then, as if by magic, we turned a corner and there, on the edge of a huge lay-by, was a little café in the middle of nowhere. What a stroke of luck! The lady behind the counter filled our water bottles while we relaxed in the coolness of the café and practised our improving language skills on her. She didn't seem to mind that we hadn't actually bought anything in there.

Coming outside some twenty minutes later, we were amazed to see a gigantic vehicle pulling into the layby. Tom counted its enormous wheels – twenty-six all together. A cylinder-shaped object of colossal proportions was mounted on top of it. We stood in awe. What on earth could it be? Part of a space rocket perhaps? And what in heaven was such a large vehicle doing here, on such a quiet little road?

As we pondered awhile with our heads bent back to take in this spectacle, in rumbled another vehicle, equally massive and also transporting a gigantic cylinder. There wasn't even time to gasp, for tearing in close behind came a canvas-topped lorry with a screech of brakes, stirring up clouds of dust. Before it had even lurched to a halt, armed soldiers were jumping down from under the canvas. They clicked their guns at the ready and encircled the vehicles, facing US! Suddenly everything had turned sinister.

We stood frozen to the spot in the café doorway, our mouths hanging open but all dry in the throat. We didn't dare take our eyes off the soldiers. What were they going to do to us? Not a word was spoken, nor a movement made. All time had stopped. Should we laugh or cry because it was all SO bizarre? Were we in imminent danger or was this some kind of farce? They were pretty formidable.

After what seemed like ages of indecision, almost bordering on panic, I began to feel defiant, then bold. Self-consciously, but with brave determination and heroism (I thought), I edged towards the bikes. The boys cautiously followed my lead, keeping close by me as we shuffled sideways, never for a moment taking our eyes off those gun-toting soldiers. Then slowly, in fear and utter silence, we turned our backs on them, swung our legs over our saddles and quietly pedalled away. They didn't shoot!

A little way along the road, when we'd gone up a hill, round a bend and had calmed down a bit, Malc said, "Let's light a banger, that'll put the wind up them!" It seemed quite a cheeky thing to do, although tinged with danger. Malc laid his bike down and, finding an old tin lying in a ditch, placed a firework inside and lit it. We stood back. The resulting 'BANG' echoed well between the hills and we were convinced that the soldiers would come tearing up the road after us, so we jumped on our bikes and pedalled like hell. They didn't. But it was amazing how we suddenly found lots of energy.

Malc had been moaning about his aching back and now resorted to walking up every single hill. At about the halfway mark, when pushing his heavy bike became too tedious, he would suggest lighting a banger. This broke the monotony and gave him some breathing space. So, together with Tom, who'd also bought bangers, they colluded to get the maximum effect from the size of firework they were lighting. If it was a small one they would try to find an old tin can to put it in. A large one could be half buried, then when it exploded, the earth would splatter all over the place, firing their imaginations with visions of landmines from the war films they had watched on television. Each time, the sounds might have differed but the effects were always the same – Malc would jump on his bike and pedal off in glee. This euphoria could last right to the top of a hill or even further; then he'd notice his backache again. Thus we continued, all the way to Châtaulin.

Pete had thought Malc and Tom to be a little childish, but now he was enjoying it every bit as much as them. I think I was too, really. It seemed pretty harmless.

We passed a camping sign about one mile before Châtaulin, but cycled past it into town, as we needed to buy provisions. The river ran along the side of the road all the way into town. It was very pretty.

Every item we bought we packed straight on to our bikes, without eating a thing. Then Pete and I took the other two boys to show them the cycle shop where we'd bought the new wheel. They were well impressed.

As it was evening, we decided to go back to the campsite we'd passed, rather than carrying on any further to look for another one. We rode up the lane and into the campsite to suss out the camping plots, passing an old brick gatehouse on the way in. We couldn't see an office anywhere.

The site seemed rather pleasant, with terraces going up the side of a hill. Each one was screened by a row of young Christmas trees. This would do nicely. The boys put up the tents behind a screen, while I set up the cooking stoves. I'd gone mad on tins today. Apart from the beef and bean cassoulet for everyone, there was a tin of mushrooms for Malc, a large tin of French beans for Pete and me, and a tin of peas and carrots for Tom. The mushrooms were in brine and turned out to be horrible and the beans were nothing to write home about, but Tom's peas and carrots were super, although Malc thought they were too sweet.

Not having seen a site office, or even looked for one, we hoped that no one would notice we were up here. Night was falling and we planned to leave quite early in the morning. If we kept our heads down maybe we wouldn't be seen.

Unfortunately, we were out of luck. A tall man came walking past with two inquisitive little puppies. They came sniffing and snuffing right up to our tent, their tails wagging ecstatically. He asked me to his office, which happened to be in the gatehouse. There, he charged me for 'deux emplacements' (I'd called it one tent), and FOUR bikes! The total was 70F. Diabolical! Was he punishing me for trying to slip in unnoticed or was he making up for not having any other customers? Now I'd really have to watch my centimes. I fondled the puppies, Cindy and Chippy, then made my way back with my own tail between my legs. That would teach me!

*   *   *   *   *

It had rained in the night, so we were packing up wet tents. In my umbrage I'd left my panniers unzipped on the bike. Now they had puddles of water inside. It wasn't a problem, I didn't carry my clothes in them. But I still felt annoyed.

We ate a giant packet of Cornflakes for breakfast and were ready to leave by 9.30 am. Good going for us! We were still fuming at having to pay so much. The boys decided they'd light a banger outside the gatehouse, on our way out. I wasn't at all keen. I didn't want the two little puppies to be frightened. So I disowned the three of them and rode off ahead up the lane.

They did their dastardly deed, then sped after me, but kept stopping to light more bangers along the lane. I was getting slightly fed up with them – the bangers and the boys!

It was exactly a week since Pete and I had hitchhiked to Châtaulin, and it was therefore market day again. The boys caught me up and we rode through the throngs of people at the market stalls, crossing the river and riding out on the other side of town. Men were busy setting up row upon row of terraced seating by the side of the road. We learned that there was to be a major cycle race the next day. No wonder we'd seen so many ace-looking cyclists racing around everywhere. One we had seen outside the cycle shop the previous day had a bike with the highest gears imaginable. How he rode up all these hills, I could not imagine.

It was a most hilly and picturesque ride today; probably the hilliest so far. These hills were long, long inclines that we could just about ride up. Then, after all the slogging to reach the top, there would be a splendid downhill swoop with wonderful views.

Near the top of one such lengthy climb we stopped at a

small shop in a place called Pont-de-Buis-lès-Quimerch. It was good to have a little break. We bought some sustenance; bananas, apples, biscuits and sweets. Pete and I bought loads of Coca-Cola sweets to keep us going. Soon the shops would be closing. Then we could keep riding without hindrance for the next two and a half hours. (They were a hindrance because they encouraged us to stop).

Now we were on the D770 again, heading for Le Faou. By the time we reached there, it was raining. What a shame! We never did get to see this little town in sunlight. (It seemed odd that this seemingly unspoilt old town should have English pop music blaring out from loudspeakers, mounted high on a wall.) After I'd shown the boys where the nice toilet was, we continued on our way.

From Le Faou we headed for Sizun, a small, agricultural town. There was still an hour to go before opening time, so we carried on towards Landivisiau.

Between Le Faou and Sizun we'd passed several huge lorries carrying aggregate. They were enormously wide loads. Preceding each lorry was a small van with its headlights on, but each van was completely covered in white dust, so the headlights were almost useless. "What a stupid way to warn us of a hazard," I said. I was glad we weren't in a car. At least, on bikes, we could jump off on to the grass verge to avoid them. Further along, we passed a gravel works and concluded that this was where the lorries had come from.

We crossed the river Elorn at least five times between Le Faou and Landivisiau. Was it meandering or were we? (This

108

river flows into the Rade de Brest between Brest and Plougastel).

To get into Landivisiau from the ring road was quite a distance. On reaching the town, we circled the centre at least twice, searching for a supermarket. By the time we'd located one it was re-opening time. I bought masses of goodies. At this rate, I would definitely be dipping into my emergency fund again. But the fruit was really cheap and looked so tempting. I went a bit overboard. I bought grapes, greengages, apricots, pears, nectarines and bananas. This was the first time I had ever eaten fresh apricots. I was disappointed. They were tasteless. Afterwards, it crossed my mind that we might all end up with diarrhoea, but fortunately we didn't.

As we'd kept to main roads all day, we had covered a much greater distance than we would have done had we meandered on the smaller roads. However the traffic became heavy after Sizun, where we joined the D30. Being a more major road, it cut through the hills rather than going over them. That, at least, was in our favour. It had been fairly cool today with light drizzle, but not enough for us to put on anoraks. It also made cycling seem less tiring and Malc hadn't complained about backache at all.

Coming out of Landivisiau, I recognised the road. It was the one we had come in on almost two weeks before. But something wasn't right about it. We soon realised what - we should have been going in the opposite direction. This town always seemed to flummox us!

It was absolutely plain sailing through Plouvorn and on

towards Roscoff, especially as the traffic had eased a little. When we reached St. Pol, Tom and Malc said they wanted to buy more bangers. They'd been working out what they could afford with the rest of their money. Not a lot! Tom had put money aside to buy SIX bottles of wine to take home. These, I think, were partly peace offerings, as he hadn't sent a single postcard to his family. The two of them went off in search of the right type of shop, while Pete and I propped our bikes up and stood in the hot sunshine. From Plouvorn onwards, the sky had become cloudless, just like on our first day here. It felt as though we were still in that same time warp.

Tom and Malc were ages and Pete and I got fed up with waiting for them. We sauntered around the town for a while. I wanted to have a look inside the cathedral, but knowing Pete wasn't all that interested, I only had a peep.

He kept saying how childish the other two were, spending all their money on French bangers. But when they came back and asked, "Are you going to buy some, Pete?" He said, "Shall I Mum?" and I told him he might as well.

We bought one or two things from our Rallye Supermarché, but not much. I was trying hard to be frugal, although I did treat the boys to a cigarette lighter each – three for 85p.

We returned to our very first campsite and were surprised to find it almost empty. The boys dropped everything and made a beeline for the beach. "Huh! That's nice," I thought. I could hear their bangers going off as I walked round the site, looking for a suitable place to put the tents. There was a stiff breeze blowing so we'd need some shelter, but this time there were no large tents to hide behind.

A high broom hedge separated the campsite from the shore. If we tucked in behind this, we'd be somewhat sheltered. When I went over to it, I was overcome by a strong smell of urine wafting up at me. But it would have to do. Nowhere else was sheltered enough.

Several times I went down to the beach to persuade the boys to come and put up their tents. In fact, before I could entice them back, I had to cook a meal. Once I'd got them there, I wouldn't let them leave until they'd finished the job. We had the same problems with the pegs as we'd had before, only this time the boys didn't have so much patience. So when an English couple arrived and erected their tent in no time at all, I went over to ask if I could borrow their hammer. According to its owner, it was a well-borrowed, well-travelled one.

Pete put his tent up first, with a little help from Tom. Most pegs needed a good hammering, but the odd one or two went straight into the sand. In such places as these, it took a couple of pegs to hold the tent secure. When they'd finished, they were free to go. I helped Malc with our tent. At our end of the plot there were fewer hammered-in pegs and more 'straight into the sand' ones. Sometimes we had to use several pegs together, to keep the tent tethered down. It was such a fiddle. Malc became impatient and left me to finish off, which was not at all his usual nature. I was really put out. It was getting dark, I was feeling cold and both my toes were sore.

When I took the hammer back to the friendly couple, they asked me in for a glass of wine, although they were still finishing their meal. I was a bit worried that our belongings were strewn about everywhere. They ought to be brought into the tents. But I thought, "Blow it! Why not?"

I was on my second mug of wine when Pete came to the door looking for me. They asked him in, and he was offered a little wine. Not long after, Malc and Tom came searching for us. They too were asked in. They had Coke.

We chatted away for ages and I was nice and warm now. Every time cycling was mentioned, John, the husband said, "You need good thighs for that", and patted mine in a very familiar fashion! So I soon avoided mentioning anything to do with bikes. He talked about one thing after another, including the war, as if he'd been there, although he certainly wasn't old enough. His voice was getting more and more slurred, while his wife, Rowena, had a permanent glazed smile. Paula, the daughter, kept giggling at them.

After my third mug, my conscience told me that we ought to get to bed, although, quite honestly, I would have been perfectly happy to stay chatting and drinking all night. So we said goodnight and went to find our belongings in the dark. That night, I had my one and only good night's sleep. Quel bon vin!

* * * * *

As usual, I was awake before Malc. I lay on my tummy, quietly writing up my diary and reminiscing about the day before. Suddenly, a huge, hairy spider raced across the page, heading straight for Malc's face. My right hand shot out instinctively to grab it. Now what was I going to do with the blessed thing? I could feel it wriggling inside my palm. I held it more tightly, hoping it wouldn't squash.

Struggling to get out of my sleeping bag one-handed, I crawled on my hand and knees to the entrance. It was so difficult to unzip the tent. It was normally a two-handed job. What a prolonged agony. I was almost gagging by the time I'd reached the central tent, where I could push up the flap and fling this monster into the hedge.

Returning to my sleeping bag, I noticed several creepy-crawlies running around the tent. Was this the consequence of leaving our stuff outside after dark? I wondered how many circuits of the tent that spider had made while we'd been asleep. Had it crawled across our faces perhaps, or, heaven forbid, even up our noses? Damn good job I'd had all that wine!

I could hear Paula riding her bike around close to our tent, whistling softly. She was trying to wake us up, I think, but I didn't respond. I wanted the boys to have a good long sleep. Tomorrow morning we'd have to start really early.

It was a gorgeous day and good for clothes drying. I washed a few items, enough to see us through to the end of the holiday and put up some clotheslines. Alas, they fell down a couple of times, being pegged in at the sandy end.

Paula was a lovely companion and kept coming over for a chat. She was ten and was missing her first week of the school term in Dartmouth.

I thought it was sad that Malc had chosen to go shopping in St. Pol on this, our last morning. It was such a beautiful day. We'd seen huge waves breaking out at sea. They were a long way off, crashing on to distant rocks, far beyond our bay. Pete and Tom wanted to see if they could reach them by walking right round the rocky peninsula.

Paula asked me if I would like to go for a swim in the sea with her and her Dad. I thought, "You need good thighs for that", and wasn't sure if I wanted to. (Luckily, I didn't have to make a decision because the whole family went off together a while later). She also asked me what we'd had for breakfast. Then I realised that we hadn't eaten much at all – just baguettes and crisps. She'd had cereals, egg on toast and toast and marmalade, and seemed amazed at our rather Spartan eating habits. Our tents fascinated her too. I told her we called it one tent, but she thought it looked more like three!

I felt slightly embarrassed that she wanted to look inside them, as by now our tent hummed of Malc's feet, since he'd been wearing his old trainers for both wet and dry pursuits. She didn't seem to notice though and loved the graffiti on the camping mats.

After I'd done all my little jobs, I laid the sleeping bags and towels over the tops of the tents to give them a good airing. I hoped they'd still be nice and dry when we packed up, early next morning.

I put on my bikini top and went to find Pete and Tom. What I really wanted to do was sunbathe on the move (to get an even tan). I set off, clambering over the plateau of four-foot high boulders, right round to the other side. Each time I rounded one headland there was another bay to walk round.

I thought it would take forever to find the boys. I doubted they could reach the enormous white horses on the horizon. Those waves were probably breaking on the Ile de Batz.

I'd reached the third bay when I suddenly remembered that I still had the ferry tickets to buy. I spun round and began to hurry back.

The tide was coming in, bringing with it lots of seaweed that hadn't been there at the beginning of our holiday. (Paula had told me that a man clears it off the beach from time to time). I went to the edge of the boulders to watch the waves lapping between them. But when the next wave came in, my foot slipped on the seaweed and disappeared between two rocks. OOH! It was SO painful. These rocks were like the roughest of rough sandpaper. Gently, I eased out my poor leg. The other was equally painful, as I'd bashed my knee as I'd gone down.

There was blood running down both legs before I reached our beach. I felt self-conscious and didn't want anyone to notice me, so I tried not to limp. In fact, there was no one about. I hobbled up the steps and sat outside the tent, feeling very sorry for myself. The grazes stung like mad and my knee was getting stiffer by the minute. I hoped I'd be able to ride my bike.

The boys all came back within the hour. There was nothing for us to eat. However, when they saw my legs, they didn't make a big fuss about food.

We'd have to go to St. Pol to stock up. Trouble was, I needed to buy the ferry tickets first. I cleaned up my legs; they were only superficially grazed and had stopped bleeding now. Then, rather stiffly, I got on the bike to see if my knee would still work for me. It wasn't so bad. Better to keep it moving.

So we set off, the boys racing ahead as usual. I shouted to Malc, who was in front of me, to catch the others up and remind them that I was going to Roscoff for the tickets first, before doing the shopping in St. Pol. Unfortunately they were nowhere to be seen in Roscoff, although they told me later that they *had* been waiting there.

At the ferry terminal there were crowds of people awaiting the departure of the 4 pm ferry. Paula and her mum and dad would be going on this one. They'd returned in the early afternoon and taken their tent down really quickly.

I wasn't allowed to buy the tickets with sterling traveller's cheques, so I had to wait for the bank to open at 3 pm. There was a long queue. I got talking to a couple from Northumberland who had also been cycling. We exchanged our experiences while we waited. They had been chased by a swarm of bees.

Now to get the tickets. I wasn't sure if I dare ask for two halves again but plucked up courage in the end. I knew we still had to pay for a night in Plymouth, as we couldn't use our rail tickets on a Saturday. I hoped I would get away with it tomorrow.

Well, that was that. Now what about shopping? I'd been gone for over an hour and didn't expect the boys to be waiting for me at St. Pol. So I decided to go straight back to the campsite. I couldn't carry all we needed by myself, anyway.

I called at the camp office to pay our camping dues, then arrived at the tent to find all three boys waiting for me. They were wondering what lovely food I'd bought for them to eat. What a disappointment! It was no use them complaining, they shouldn't have dashed off like that.

Right! We would *have* to go shopping now. But I couldn't face going all the way to the St. Pol supermarket. It would have to be the slightly more expensive stores in Roscoff. However, when we got there Pete and Malc said they had to go over to St. Pol for their final purchase of bangers. Tom and I would have to manage without them. My own sons were letting me down now!

Tom followed me back and forth to various shops to help me find the best bargains. Earlier he'd bought five bottles of wine to take home. Now I helped him out with his sixth bottle; cider this time. We bought food for the evening, food for breakfast (although we'd have to be up extremely early to eat it) and food for the ferry. Secretly, I hoped we'd have some of the ferry food left when we reached Plymouth. It was lucky for me that Tom had two empty panniers on his bike for all these purchases. We loaded up and rode back to the site.

I told the boys that we should pack up as much as possible before dark, as we'd be leaving the site by 6.30 am the next day, before daybreak. But after our dinner they went straight down to the beach with their bangers and didn't return until well after nightfall. We went to bed, setting the alarm for 5 am.

Rough crossing

Roscoff to Plymouth

The wind was terrific in the night, making the tents flap like kites. I don't think I slept much, especially when the rain came down, adding to the noise. By 3 am our tent was sagging. Malc was soon awake; the wind and rain were on his side and he was getting wet. We realised that the tent was tilting. Every gust of wind was wiggling the pole further into the sand, making the sides cave in. Hanging on to it, we burst out laughing. What a predicament! We decided we might as well get up; we couldn't lie down. Pete was awake now. His tent wasn't collapsing, but he was pretty sure the rain would be getting in on Tom's side, and Tom was fast asleep.

I dressed in my usual 'going away' outfit and began to gather my belongings together in the tent. I might as well keep my stuff dry. Malc's torch batteries were fading fast. Soon we were in pitch darkness, groping around. I rolled my sleeping bag and mat around the drum bag of clothes (by feel) and tied it all up with string. After I'd put it into a dustbin bag, I chucked it outside, out of the way. Then Malc and I did the same with

118

his wet sleeping bag and mat. He would have to take them out of the dustbin bag later, to roll round his tent, after we'd taken it down.

Pete did the same in his tent, in between lending us his torch to find things. Tom woke up and swore profusely when he felt the state of his bed. His clean shorts and other clothes were laid on top of his sleeping bag, ready to wear on the ferry. They were getting wet.

It had stopped raining now. We waited for the alarm to go off. It was late – by a couple of minutes! It would be good to get the tents down quickly, while it was fine, but Pete and Malc surprised me, by firstly nipping over to the toilet block with their wash bags. Had they become more self conscious about the way they looked since the French girls in Bénodet had shown an interest in them? Anyway, they were soon back. Pete's batteries had run out now.

He and Malc had seen two shooting stars. Tom and I missed them. We were still in the tents at the time.

When Malc and I took our tent down, we found that nearly all the pegs had come out on his side. Tom's torch soon gave up as well, so we worked by the light of a lighthouse, which was flashing every few seconds. It was very eerie.

It seemed a stupid idea to bother with cornflakes and milk now, although that had been the intention. Instead, I thought perhaps we ought to have a cupful of Benco each, to use up the milk. But none of us felt like it and I didn't really want to get the cooker out at this stage. It was about 6am and still pitch dark.

So I had an unopened packet of cornflakes, a litre of milk and half a jar of Benco to carry, together with all the other ferry food I'd packed the night before. The haversacks would be really heavy. We shared a litre of orange juice between our four bottles, spilling much of it because we couldn't see properly. Scrabbling around on our hands and knees, we felt for any spare tent pegs we might have missed. It took ages to find the little bag we kept them in.

Now we had to strap the big rolls on top of the panniers. It was bad enough that we couldn't lean the bikes against anything, but fastening bungees on in the dark was even trickier. Still, we were more 'au fait' by now.

It was 6.30 am and in spite of everything we were on time. The boys waited outside the toilets while I had a quick cat-lick at the washbasins, hoping I'd look decent in daylight. Two cars crept slowly past us. We knew where they were heading!

We rode in convoy to Roscoff, down the middle of the road to miss the puddles and potholes. I led the way with my front dynamo light. Malc brought up the rear because his back light was still working. We crept slowly along as only I could see what the surface of the road was like. It was raining again.

Thankfully, we made it to the terminal without mishap and I looked for a kiosk where I could change the tickets for boarding cards. There wasn't one. I wondered what sort of system they had here. Might I get caught out?

The rain was bucketing down, so much so that a spout of water was shooting off the roof of the foyer. I held the tickets under it for a while, hoping to obliterate the writing a little.

I told the boys not to stand near me while I went into Enquiries, feeling a bit of a criminal by now. But at the counter I was given four 'Brittany Ferry' stickers instead of boarding cards, and they didn't question me at all.

The boys took a sticker each. Malc and Tom immediately stuck theirs on their foreheads, then various other unmentionable places before they finally left them under their anoraks. So far so good, but I didn't know the procedures this side of the Channel.

Luckily there was a small sheltered area at the head of the queue. We went up and stood under it with several other cyclists, none of whom looked as bedraggled as we did. There was no sign of Liz and Ian. We wondered where they could be.

Cars were streaming off the ferry in the rain. We waited ages behind huge grilled gates, like animals in a cage, desperate to get out. Several official-looking men stood amongst us, wearing the typical long beige French raincoats. When at last they unlocked the gates, we cyclists seemed to be on starting blocks. With all the pushing and confusion, our nearest official-man didn't even ask to see my tickets. He just glanced briefly at our passports as we prepared for take-off. The gates opened wide and we all rushed down to the ferry. Phew!

As we fastened our bikes up we kept scanning the entrance for Liz and Ian. We hoped they were OK.

For some reason, we made a beeline for the same lounge area as before and sat on the front row in the very same seats. We were soaked from head to foot, feeling cold and worn out. Lots of French cleaners were emptying bins and still tidying up from the last crossing. We noticed that the man folding blankets wore a special apron which made him look more superior to the other cleaners. There was a hippy fellow a few seats away, huddled in a blanket and almost asleep. A lady vacuuming nearby couldn't get round his feet. She kept giving us black looks as she thought we were taking the mickey out of her. But we weren't laughing at *her*. We were just watching all the people coming up the stairs in front of us and making comments about them. We couldn't help giggling from time to time, being in a silly mood.

A middle-aged couple came and sat behind us. Then they got up again to take some sick bags from a dispenser on the wall. We laughed. But they said, "You wait, you'll be wanting some soon." I suddenly remembered our sickness tablets. Malc, Tom and I swallowed two each, washing them down with orange juice. Pete didn't need any; he never seemed to get sick.

We were starving hungry, but I refused to cut the bread for sandwiches while sitting on the front row, on show. The boys would be obliged to come to the back row with me if they wanted food. As I drew out a long gingerbread cake from the haversack, they all decided they'd rather have that, instead of sandwiches. Good! It was already cut into slices. It was lush and there were *five* slices each.

We were getting bored with waiting. Through the back windows we could see lorry after lorry still boarding. It was nearly 8.30 am. We should have left half an hour before.

Out on the back deck was a group of six German men in identical jackets. They were obviously photographers, as they had complicated cameras slung on their shoulders, with lots of spare lenses. They fussed and faffed about, trying to get different lenses out of their shoulder bags with one hand while precariously holding on to their precious cameras with the other. The gusts of wind were so terrific that it was nearly blowing them over. It was like watching clowns on a trapeze. However, they seemed determined to photograph the rusty iron girders at the ferry mounting point. It had stopped raining now.

"Votre attention, s'il vous plait," came the lady's voice on the tannoy. She proceeded to tell us in French first, then English, that if the alarm sounded a certain number of times, all passengers must assemble at emergency points, where crew members would issue life-jackets and give them instructions. Also, no one would be allowed out on deck once we left port, and all the doors would be locked. We were suddenly very quiet and worried. Images of the Zeebrugge disaster flashed through our minds, with visions of that stricken ferry keeling over on its side and sinking. Still, that had been nothing to do with weather conditions (the lower doors hadn't been shut properly). We mustn't be morbid.

At last the engines started, although you could barely hear them up here at the top. As we drew out of port we noticed that some people were still outside on deck. We wondered when they'd be brought inside and locked in, but they weren't.

We didn't have to travel many metres to feel the sea. There were white horses from horizon to horizon. Soon the ferry was rearing and dipping over huge waves. Within half an hour I had to grab a sick bag from a wall dispenser and dash outside to perform. Malc was right behind me. What a waste of that lovely ginger cake, and the tablets of course. But now I felt much better and went back inside. Tom got up and headed for the toilets.

A quarter of an hour later I had to rush outside again, feeling dreadful. Malc was still out there, resting his head on the rail. How on earth could we put up with five and a half more hours of this? If we had been on a fairground ride, like the waltzers, we could have climbed off after a few minutes. But here there was no escape.

I noticed that the waste bins out on deck were already three-quarters full. They must have forgotten to empty them after the previous crossing. So after my third session outside, I decided that from now on I'd better use the ladies' toilets instead.

When I next ventured out, the deck was filling up with sick folk. They had unstacked the chairs and were sitting in the sun. But it was so windy out there and in wet clothes I felt freezing. I went back inside. Pete had gone. After sitting in the lounge for a while I realised that the televisions made me feel worse. Soon I was reeling and rolling up to the toilets again, being thrown from one side of the gangway to the other as the ferry pitched and lurched. I kept seeing the same faces. We exchanged woeful looks – even managed to smile at our predicament, sometimes.

The smells just churned me up. If I went outside I could smell diesel fumes. If I went into the toilets the chemical smell got to me. In the lounge I felt claustrophobic and the tellies drove me mad. I sat down for a while with a bag handy, trying to calm myself. But it was no good. I would have to go outside and put up with being cold and smelling the diesel fumes.

Malc was still out there, feeling rotten. He said he was going inside to lie on the floor and make himself go to sleep. Now that our stomachs were virtually empty, one bag lasted for ages.

Seated on the deck, I tried to go blank. As my trousers and shoes dried off, I began to warm up a little. It was such a beautiful day out there, but not on this bucking bronco of a ferry.

If the chairs had been more enveloping I would definitely have gone to sleep. But as it was, my head would suddenly loll forwards with a jolt, bringing me back to reality. Then, after a few lurches of the ferry and a few whiffs of the diesel, I was feeling rotten all over again. In between, I was managing a little conversation with the lady next to me. She could remember being on a much worse crossing than this. She said she had laid her little boy down on the deck and couldn't have cared less what had happened to him.

A family behind us were discussing what food they were going to buy. "Shut up, for goodness sake!" I muttered under my breath as they headed for the café.

Pete came along and sat down, next to me. Even he had been sick twice. He didn't know I was out there. He'd been sitting just around the corner for ages.

As we came closer to England the sea became less rough. Pete went inside for a coffee. He came back to tell me that it was much less rocky two flights down in the café. I wasn't sure if I'd be able to stomach the smell, but went along with him all the same.

We sat looking out of the windows, which were spattered with what I'd thought at first, to be bird muck, but wasn't. Soon I began to feel ever so slightly better, but Pete wasn't helping much, first diving into our bag of popcorn, then having a salad baguette.

When I'd improved enough, I thought I'd try to persuade Malc to come down. He refused and went back to sleep. Pete and I bought some coffee from the machine. It was awful and I couldn't drink mine.

It wasn't until we arrived in England that we saw Tom again. Apparently he'd fallen asleep in the gents' toilets and had been awoken by a bang on the head. An irate German had forced the door open!

We hung about as before, not wanting to be stuck in the fumes while all the cars were being driven off. But when we saw that a cyclist was first out, we hurried down for our bikes.

There was a small black cloud hanging directly over Plymouth and it was raining, while all around was blue sky.

It seemed harder to adapt to riding on the left again than it had been to get used to the right. Cars were streaming out of the terminal car park. It was so congested that I felt quite unsafe. Buses and taxis whizzed by on the inside bus lane, and cars changed lanes in front of us. We were all following Pete to the railway station. I don't know how he knew which way to go – he must have seen a sign somewhere. Before we could decide where to spend the night, we needed to know the train times for tomorrow.

The man I asked in the booking office said there was a train at 3.30 pm. But I told him we couldn't travel until tomorrow. "Oh, got a Blue Saver have you?" he asked. Then he told me that we could travel on a Saturday now because it was after September 1st. That was such good news. The thought of managing a night in Plymouth had been nagging me, as I was really reluctant to dip into my telephone money again (there was bound to be a red reminder waiting at home).

So we went straight off to find the platform. Again, we ended up on the wrong side. But we soon got it right and found four more cyclists who were waiting to go to Gloucester.

When the train arrived it was crowded. There was no chance of getting eight bikes on. In fact they couldn't even take a group of four. All we could do was wait for another one.

Nearby was a porters' office. The porters were most concerned that we should all get home safely that day. They looked at their timetables. A train for Milton Keynes was due at 5.30 pm, which would be going through Cheltenham. Next they checked on the computer to see what luggage it was carrying. Yes, there was enough room for all our bikes. What a handy system!

We sat on a railway seat, where I cut the bread to make sandwiches. The crumbs went everywhere. I was so glad I hadn't attempted this on the ferry. Nice as the railway staff were, they frowned a bit at the mess we made. But the pigeons appreciated it. What they left, I swept under the seat with my foot.

At last the train came in. It was half empty; plenty of room for the bikes and for each of us to have a double seat to ourselves.

The journey was superb and soporific, but I forced myself to stay awake, as I didn't want to miss an inch of scenery. The sky was cloudless and the landscape looked beautiful. I almost wondered why we'd gone to France in the first place, especially since that awful crossing. Then I reflected on what a great experience it had been for all of us. We'd enjoyed ourselves so much. It would be fantastic to go again, to explore another part. If only money grew on trees!

Well, all I wished now was that we'd be able to get from Cheltenham to Stroud without any hassle. I wondered what the guardsman would be like. Not that big, horrible bloke we'd encountered before, I hoped.

A jovial looking ticket collector came along and checked our tickets. "Where are the children?" he asked. I pointed behind. He looked at me in disbelief. When I told him their ages, he said, "Blimey, what on earth do you feed them on?" "Weetabix" I said.

We had our first cup of tea for seventeen days. It wasn't a very good one, but the novelty was nice.

By the time we had reached Cheltenham it was almost dark. We didn't know if there would be a train to Stroud at that time of night. The thought of cycling there in the dark made us cringe, especially as we were fairly whacked out. Besides, we were rather short on lights, so it wouldn't be very safe. But as it happened, there was a train due in two hours' time.

The Gloucester cyclists said they were going to get pedalling, as they couldn't bear to hang about any longer.

Lucky things. They didn't have many miles to go, and it was a flat run for them.

I thought a dose of fish and chips would do us all good. We found a chip shop just across the road from the station. Unfortunately, I did have to dip into my telephone money this time, so I asked Tom if he would mind contributing his last 75p towards our supper. For some reason, that seemed to really upset him. He went in and bought a small portion of chips for himself, then sat alone outside to eat them. My intention had been to pay the extra money towards his fish and chips. He'd really got the hump. I felt awful eating mine in front of him but to ease my conscience a little, I bought him a sachet of tomato sauce.

I phoned Jim, who promised to meet us. He said he'd ring Tom's dad to tell him what time we expected to arrive. Tom was hoping that his dad would meet him with his pick-up truck. Then he could just hoist his bike into the back and ride home in comfort. I think, secretly, we all hoped Tom's dad might offer to take our bikes as well. Then we could *all* ride home in comfort.

I felt a little nervous waiting for this train, hoping they'd let us on. The train due into the station before the Stroud one was running late. I wondered whether that train or ours would arrive first. Then I reflected that if ours came in first and we took ages getting our bikes on, the other one might run into the back of us. Pete told me not to be silly; everything was computerised, now.

The other train came and went. Ours was soon after; same platform but opposite direction!

A rather small black man wearing large spectacles poked

his head out of the goods van at the front. He waved his arms to tell us to go to the back of the train, quickly. At least, that's what we supposed he was telling us (although, from this distance, it was hard to tell whether he was beckoning us or shooing us). We raced to the back of the train all the same. Pete got there first and tried to open the goods-van door. It would only open a few inches. He pulled and pulled. Then he tried to pull open the adjacent, much wider door. That wouldn't budge either.

We looked up the platform to see that the little black man was still waving his arms at us. Pete had another go. This time I helped. Tugging with all our might, we at last managed to force open the thin, right-hand door. It didn't seem possible that we could squeeze our loaded bikes through such a narrow gap but we had to try. Breathlessly, we rammed and pushed until, eventually, all four bikes were on board. What a relief.

A porter came to close the door behind us. But now it wouldn't shut. He slammed and bashed it, to no avail, so he came inside to pull it. Still no luck! The doors just wouldn't line up properly. Then he noticed that the hinges on the left-hand door were completely off their mountings.

What had we done? Why, if there was a porter here now, couldn't he have helped us when we needed him? The little guard rushed down the platform to see what all the commotion was about. He found a crowbar and began to thrash at the broken door. The result was that he bent the screws over at right angles. If he'd calmly lined them up to the screw-holes in the frame, he'd probably have managed to secure the door. But no, this ham-fisted little chap knew best. Give him his due, though, he didn't say a single cross word to *us*, although his face looked like thunder. Another man explained to us that the left-hand door has to be opened inwards first, to allow the right-hand door to open outwards. If only we'd known!

They were getting no joy and told us, crossly, to go and sit down; we weren't supposed to be in the goods wagon anyway. We found some seats just inside the next carriage but weren't able to see what was going on. We wondered if this train would ever be ready to leave.

The next time we looked out of the window we saw that the carriage door was laid out on a platform seat. Blimey! They were taking the train to bits. A phone on the wall started ringing. The railway worker, who answered, had to explain why the train hadn't left yet.

Nobody spoke to us, but sitting opposite were three railway workers who were going off duty. In low voices they discussed the situation, talking out of the sides of their mouths and giving us sidelong glances. They seemed to think this train might have to be cancelled and we'd all be put onto another train. Apparently, people would now miss their connections in Swindon. We felt terrible.

After the longest twenty-five minutes we'd ever endured, the train was ready to go. I was thinking to myself, ''What if the door comes off when we get out at Stroud?'' So I kept my fingers tightly crossed.

At Gloucester the little bespectacled man left the train. Thank goodness. At least he wouldn't be around if we made another cock-up.

Very soon we arrived in Stroud. A smiley, round-faced guardsman greeted us in the guard's van. He explained that since the train had left Gloucester station backwards, we would be getting out on the opposite side. Oh, what a relief!

We bundled out to find Tom's new stepmother and Jim waiting anxiously on the platform, wondering what on earth all the delay had been about. Tom was disappointed because his dad wasn't there with the pick-up truck - we all were. But never mind, we'd made it, and that was the main thing.

Taking the loads off our bikes we put them into their respective cars. Then in convoy again, because of our lack of lights, we rode out of Stroud. As we peeled off to the right for Butterrow, we shouted "Cheerio" to Tom. He carried straight on into the darkness, heading for Thrupp with no lights at all. It was such a casual parting after all we'd been through together. We ought to have been having a party.

Pete and Malc came racing by me up the hill, leaving me alone in the dark. Suddenly I felt so tired, I just had to get off and walk. Normally, I wouldn't dream of walking up here on my own at this time of night.

As I reached the sharp bend over the railway bridge, I glanced briefly into the shadowy bushes on the railway embankment and shivered. This was the spookiest spot for me. Then, rounding the steep corner into the last straight, I was confronted by a dazzling full moon, pouring its cold brightness all down the hill. Now it seemed as if I was walking up a silver river in a trance. Would life ever be the same again?

* * * * *

PART TWO

SUMMER 1988

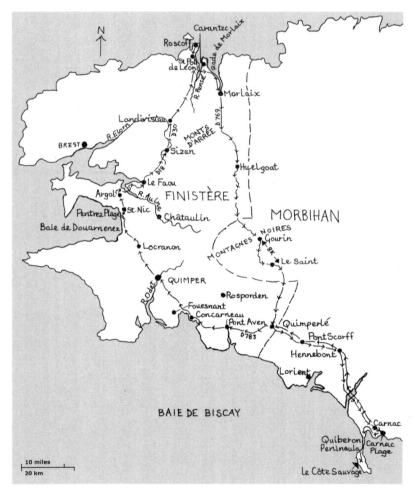

Brittany 1988

After that holiday in 1987, I hadn't thought it possible that we could go away again. When you're constantly struggling to make ends meet, holidays seem an impossible extravagance. But I never stopped hoping. Truth to tell, I was keener than ever to get away and have some adventure. Besides, we now had all the equipment.

Scrimping and saving had become such a habit that I couldn't break the addiction. If I had any odd change left over, I squirreled it away in my little tin in the kitchen drawer, just like the previous year. If a friend needed curtains altering, a room painting or their house cleaned ready for guests, I was there to earn a little money.

Then in the spring, Jim's dad had a stroke. He was in a bad way, and it seemed we wouldn't be going anywhere. But summer arrived in a continuous squall of cold winds and showers and we couldn't help remembering the sunny, fun-filled times we'd spent in Brittany.

By August Grandad had improved no end, enough for us to consider going away after all, though we didn't have quite the same enthusiasm.

Pete now had an evening job, so Malc had taken over his paper round. Maybe the boys might contribute. Wishful thinking, perhaps.

As well as his regular evening job, Pete had managed to find a holiday job. But his spending had increased with his expanding ambitions; he'd chosen to replace all the components on his bike with new racing parts. If all went to plan, he would transfer these to the new racing frame he hoped to buy next year. He'd also become very fashion conscious. He could barely fulfil his own needs.

He'd been good enough, however, to transfer his old gears on to Malc's bike, so with an extension now fitted to the handlebar stem, at least Malc's machine was sorted.

Me? I still had the old hand-painted bike with five gears. At least the frame hadn't cracked up yet. By now I'd put battery lights on both the front and rear (dynamos make pedalling hard work). In a moment of optimism I'd bought myself two pairs of lightweight lace-ups from a sale in the club book. They were just about suitable for cycling, and a size bigger to avoid putting pressure on my toes.

There would be just the three of us this year. Tom wasn't on the scene anymore. I'd probably put him off camping (and economising) for good. Apart from the fact that we'd only have one little camping stove between us, we didn't think it would make too much difference.

Once again, sunny Brittany was beckoning.

Return to Brittany

Stroud, Thursday August 18 1988

At least it wasn't raining. That was a good start. We had shopping to do, plus many unfinished tasks. Jim took me to town fairly early and I hoped that by the time we got home Pete and Malc would be all packed up, ready to go.

Pete, who was now 16, would need his own passport this year. He was going to pay for it himself, although he hadn't bought it yet. I was cross that he'd left it until the last minute, but he told me not to worry. He'd have it all sorted by the time I got home.

Shopping took much longer than expected because the local camping shop didn't have the tethering rubbers that I thought I should buy. The original ones were beginning to perish. So we had to drive out to a large camping centre to find some. I must say, it was rather remiss of *me* to leave it this late.

We didn't arrive home until midday. Pete was standing at the front door looking agitated. "Where the heck have you been all this time?" he said. "I can't get my passport until they've seen my birth certificate. Where is it?"

He'd already been down to the Post Office twice. The first time he'd discovered he didn't have enough money in the bank. The second time (after first coming all the way home for some cash) they'd asked to see his birth certificate. Consequently he'd spent the rest of the morning waiting for us.

Although he was chomping at the bit, I persuaded him to have a bite to eat before he went back down to Stroud. We found the certificate and off he sped. 'Third time lucky,' I hoped.

While he was gone I phoned Cheltenham station to check the time of the train and make sure there was room for the bikes on board. There was. The train was due to leave at 5.35 pm. This year we intended to cycle to Cheltenham, giving ourselves plenty of time (we couldn't cope with another scenario like last year, when they had refused to take our bikes on the train at Stroud station). However, the thought of cycling up and over the Cotswold edge to get there didn't thrill me at all, even though Jim was going to take our luggage in the car.

Malc had packed his panniers. I helped him roll up his tent and bedding and tie a cord tightly round them. We put the roll inside a dustbin liner. There was no feeling of excitement as there had been last year.

Outside it began to rain. No sign of Pete. Malc helped me roll up my stuff then we put both our rolls inside their bright-red covers. Still no sign of Pete, and he had everything to pack yet.

The phone rang. It was Jim's friend, John, from down the lane. When he heard we were planning to cycle to Cheltenham, he offered to assist us by driving *his* car there as well. Great news. With both cars, we'd hopefully be able to squeeze the bikes, baggage and ourselves in, without doing any cycling. What a relief.

It was still raining; the sort of rain that goes on and on with no break in the clouds. Where was that Pete? How the heck did he think he was going to get everything ready in time?

John came round to see how things were going. He was cheery and jollied us along. Eventually Pete turned up, drenched.

"Where the devil have you *been*? Have you got your passport?" This time it was *me* standing at the front door looking worried. "Yes," he replied casually. "This rain's really refreshing." How could he be so laid back? As far as he knew we still had to cycle all the way to Cheltenham. He'd only been queuing for a haircut.

I regretted telling him that John had offered us a lift, because he took forever to get ready, messing with this, adjusting that and rearranging the other. In the end we were panicking and had to rush to Cheltenham, even in cars.

We arrived with fifteen minutes to spare. While the men and boys unloaded the bikes, I dashed inside to queue for tickets. It was I who was chomping at the bit now. At last it was my turn.

"No, you can't have tickets from Stroud," I was told, "because the ticket machine will automatically print 'Cheltenham' on them." That was a damn nuisance. It would mean we might have to cycle back to Stroud on our return journey, probably late at night.

I gathered up my tickets, money, railcard, passport and all

the other essentials that I'd dragged out of my bag in a hurry, and carefully carried them to a spare windowsill. I sorted them out as quickly as possible.

That was odd. I only had five tickets. One of the return tickets was missing. I went through everything several times in great haste, looking inside the passport cover, checking my pockets, retracing my footsteps and searching the floor. It was nowhere. I couldn't have been given it. I rushed back to the queue. There were two people in front of me. The train must surely be imminent. I was getting very hot.

The ticket man was adamant that he'd given me all the tickets because the machine would automatically print out two of each, for returns. "Don't worry, you can buy another one in Plymouth on your return journey. Anyway it's bound to turn up."

Jim and John came in, wondering what the extra panic was about. It was pointless to worry about the ticket now; we had a train to catch. The bikes were ready to wheel down to the platform. We just had time.

5.35 pm came and went. Then the tannoy announced that the train was running half an hour late. Jim and John hung on, shivering in the shorts they were wearing in defiance of the weather. It felt as if we were standing in a wind tunnel in the middle of winter. "You'll be all right now won't you?" asked Jim, hopefully. "Do you mind if we go?"

We didn't. We said our farewells, then sat on a trolley to wait. I didn't feel an atom of enthusiasm. Maybe it was the result of the last few months worrying about Grandad, or perhaps it was guilt that I was leaving the problems behind.

It might just be because the weather was so bloody awful. It could only get better.

Our train drew in at 6.15 pm, creeping slowly past us along the edge of the platform until it filled the whole length from end to end. It was hard not to feel a slight twinge of excitement as this long snake of a train arrived all the way from Aberdeen. We had no trouble getting the bikes on board and were soon warm and cosy in our seats, looking forward to sunnier climes.

Our plan this year was to catch the 8 am ferry the next morning. Earlier, Malc had made me promise that we'd find a campsite for the night, in order to get a decent night's sleep. Now I was putting up a front, because in my heart I knew it was unlikely that I could fulfil this promise. I couldn't. Our late train arrived in Plymouth in pitch darkness, and it was raining.

We alighted onto platform 7, feeling tired. Seeing two lads with mountain bikes heading towards the foyer, we followed them to see where they might be spending the night. We found them searching the adverts on the wall, looking for bed and breakfast accommodation.

"Are you catching the ferry in the morning?" I asked. No they weren't, but they needed to get a good bed for the night, as tomorrow they'd be cycling to Land's End.

In the foyer was a map of Plymouth. We went through the motions of looking for campsites on it, although we knew that camping was out of the question now. Luckily we couldn't find a single one. So with no other option, we left the lads in the foyer, still scanning for B&Bs, and decided we'd have to sleep in the waiting room we'd seen between platforms 7 and 8.

We found two waiting rooms next to each other. The first was fairly modern with long, padded seats covered in plastic. But it was lit very brightly by fluorescent lights. No way could we sleep with that brightness. Next to it was a smaller, old-fashioned room that was more dimly lit. At my suggestion we went in there.

The seats were wooden and reminded me of church pews, not half as comfortable as the ones next door. There was a seat across the bottom wall, with a seat on each side of it. There, a plump young man had staked his claim. He was sprawled across the middle seat, complete with his own overhead electric fire plus its personal switch cord. We would have to make do with the opposite, cold end of the room, where two seats faced his.

Malc curled up on the farthest seat, which left Pete and me to share the other. It was very uncomfortable and quite chilly. I asked Pete if he'd mind unpacking a pair of his socks for me to wear. My legs were getting really cold. I was wearing calf-length trousers and regretting it, and I couldn't get to my own clothes without completely taking my roll to bits.

Sometime before midnight a train drew in and the young man departed. Pete jumped into the hot seat, while Malc and I took up residence on the two seats either side of him. None of the seats was long enough to stretch our legs out, but we made a serious attempt to get some sleep. We'd already taken the rolls off the bikes to use as pillows.

I had an added bonus. This year I'd treated myself to a padded beach-mat which, when folded in four, made a flat-pack bag. It was going to provide extra padding under my hips and I could start using it now. But I found it didn't make much difference. I just couldn't get comfy. Pete dozed off for a while.

The seats were so hard that it was necessary to turn over quite frequently. This meant moving the pillows from one end of the seat to the other every single time, and in my case, hiding my bum-bag securely under the roll, in case I fell asleep. The whole process took away any feelings of sleepiness. It didn't feel like the start of a holiday at all.

* * * * *

I was surprised to wake up and find that I'd actually been to sleep. Surprised also to see that another fat fellow had joined us. He was fast asleep in a most ungainly fashion, on the seat that Pete and I had first occupied. Malc and I looked at each other and grinned but I could tell from Malc's strained face that he wasn't getting any sleep.

Trains came and went. The porters seemed to derive a lot of fun from their night shifts. From time to time they would gather in a large group on one of the far platforms, waiting for a mail train. A steady drone of voices could be heard, broken by sudden outbursts of raucous laughter (I suppose that's what had woken me up). As each train arrived it blocked the porters from our view, but we could hear them loading the mail sacks onto their trolleys and wheeling them away. With the job completed, the train would glide away like a theatre curtain, revealing the platform once more, empty and uncannily silent.

That was the time to close your eyes and try to sleep. But the fat fellow was fascinating us. Only a porky person could relax in those funny positions on a wooden bench. With his legs dangling over the arm at one end and his head hanging right back over the other, he began to snort like a pig. Malc and I were creased up; laughing but trying not to make a sound. Our sides were aching.

Daylight became dimly apparent. We felt great relief, knowing that at long last morning was approaching. It had been really hard work trying to sleep here. We hung on a bit longer and kept craning our necks to see what sort of weather was in store. But it was far too early to tell. Everywhere was dark grey.

We were as stiff as boards when we stood up, and took ages to get going. Malc told me he'd stayed awake all night. "One of us had to keep an eye on the bikes," he said dolefully. Poor kid, he looked worn out, while I'd been feeling pleased with myself for actually falling asleep.

I wandered outside to get a better picture of the weather situation. There wasn't much sky space between the platform roofs, but I could see clouds scudding by. Down here on the platform the air felt quite still. When the boys asked me what it was like I didn't mention the wind. It would only start Malc worrying about the ferry crossing. Since our very rough crossing last year, Malc had vowed *never* to go on a ferry again. He'd conceded slightly, saying he'd only go on the shortest route possible. But with a little bribery and a lot of persuasion, I'd managed to make him change his mind. I'd also assured him that very few crossings would be as rough as last year's, especially in summertime.

It was almost 6 am. We might as well strap our rolls back onto the bikes and make our way to the ferry terminal.

We walked past the other waiting room. It was now in complete darkness. Could it be? Surely not! We went back and peered through the windows. Well, blow me! Stretched out on the padded seats and fast asleep, were the two mountain-bike boys. Oh, the envy we felt. If only we'd known that *we* could have switched off those bright lights, we would gladly have slept in there. I could have kicked myself. I bet the boys would like to have done so too.

It didn't take us long to get to the ferry terminal. There was hardly any traffic and we vaguely remembered the way from last year. I bought 'open return' tickets without having to wait, then went over to the bank counter and changed our money into francs. Everything was going surprisingly smoothly, which helped me keep calm, for Malc's sake.

In the café we had a cup of tea and a Kit-Kat each, and relaxed as we began to warm up. We'd made a decision not to eat very much before the crossing, in case it all got wasted.

Outside it was fairly breezy, but I didn't think it would be enough to affect the crossing. Malc and I took travel sickness tablets anyway.

We stayed in the café for ages, just gazing vacantly into space, half asleep. But as people began arriving, the hum of their voices and the scraping of chairs awoke us from our reverie.

Pete looked at his watch. There was still another hour to go. He went over to a shop in the corner and came back with a crossword book. That seemed like a good idea. I followed suit and chose a puzzle book. It would give us something to do during the crossing. I spotted a booklet about Brittany, showing all the places of interest to visit. I dipped into my meagre savings and bought that as well. Maybe this year, we could fit a little more sightseeing into our tour.

There'd been some tightening of security this year. Our passports were closely scrutinised, unlike last time.

We were amongst the first passengers to board the ferry. We tied up the bikes ourselves because this time the crew members were too busy elsewhere. Then for some unknown reason, we made our way to exactly the same place as last year. We just wanted to be sure we had seats.

Within half an hour of leaving port it was evident that the sea was rough. Not so terribly rough as last year, but bad enough. Malc wanted to lie down on the floor, which would help him overcome his seasickness. But as no one else was lying down, he didn't dare. He thought that maybe it wasn't allowed on daytime crossings.

We went out on deck to get the fresh air, swaying down the metal staircase. Very few people were outside, which wasn't surprising, considering the chill in the air. There were loads of empty seats, many of them still in stacks. The most sheltered spot we could find was with our backs to the restaurant, directly below the lounge. I tried to take Malc's mind off feeling sick by reading extracts from my Brittany booklet to him. But I could tell he wouldn't last much longer.

I hurried up to the lounge for some sick bags. There weren't any. That was a nuisance. So I dashed down two flights to the information desk in the café and asked for some there. They didn't have any either but said they would send for some. As I stood there, waiting and waiting, I began to feel ill myself. I asked again, probably looking rather pukey by now because they gave me a plastic bag to be going on with.

A man came rushing through the café carrying a vomiting child under his arm horizontally, like a battering ram. They headed towards the toilets leaving a trail of sick splashes all along the nice new carpet. The sight churned me up, especially as it was in the café.

I was worried about Malc and hoped he'd be coping. But it was no use going back without any bags.

At last a man came by, filling up the sick-bag dispensers along the wall. I grabbed a handful and feeling quite grotty now, heaved myself up the stairs and back out on deck. Malc had gone. I couldn't see him anywhere. Well at least I had some bags for him, next time. This year, they were flimsy plastic ones. I didn't fancy them at all. I much preferred the paper variety. "Anything's better than nothing," I thought, as I placed my first see-through bag into the bin.

Pete and I sat glumly looking out to sea. Even he was queasy now. In fact the whole deck was filling up with sick people. No sign of Malc, though. We didn't know where he was, though as we got more and more engrossed in our own nausea we didn't much care.

An odd group seated themselves next to us. It took us ages to work out that they were all one family. There were three fair-haired boys, the eldest about Pete's age. He took Malc's seat and sat almost facing us. The middle boy looked about Malc's age – fourteen - and the youngest, about ten. Their mother was seated next to me.

Near them was a tall, swarthy man, who never sat down and only spoke to them in a foreign language. They replied quite casually in English, as if it was the most normal thing in the world to do. Pete told me that the man was Spanish, so I took his word for it. It was good for us to have this distraction. We were fascinated by how the boys listened in one language and answered in the other. They had weird names, not foreign ones, but improbable ones.

We sat there for ages, shivering, being sick and eavesdropping. The wind was sending spray across the deck with each wave that broke on the bow, making us quite damp. Loads of people were coddled in blankets. I was very grateful when Pete offered to fetch me one. I felt rooted to my seat; too cold and worn out to bother to move. Being wrapped in blankets cheered us up slightly. There was such a lot going on now that time seemed to be passing more quickly.

A sudden clatter of clogs on the metal steps made everyone's eyes turn towards the staircase. A young girl was rushing down on some urgent quest. Too late! She didn't make it. Jerking her head over the side, she cascaded vomit into the wind. An unlucky group of people who had been huddling under the stairs tried to leap out of the way but were caught anyway, as the wind blew it all back again.

The staircase was now decorated in the stuff. We witnessed countless people descending the steps who unwittingly slid a hand down the banister then wiped it onto their clothes, thinking it was just water.

A little while later, a couple came on deck with their toddler son, feeling very proud of him as he clambered on the bottom steps. They smiled and peep-bowed to him through the gaps. Nobody, not even us, had the decency to tell them what he was crawling in.

Out here was now like a veranda in a nursing home; so many putty-faced people sitting around in blankets. The floor of the deck had become wet and slippery, which made it hazardous to cross, especially with the ferry lurching up and down all the time. We couldn't help chuckling though, watching the different ways that people walked across it. There were those who stooped in a drunken fashion, keeping their bodies close to the deck, while others would take a straight, stiff-legged attitude, rocking from side to side, occasionally doing a little syncopated chasse to one side or the other, to keep their balance.

The eldest son of the family next to us was having a very intellectual conversation with his mother about geology and coal mining. Every so often he would heave over his sick bag, then say in a very loud voice, "What will it feel like when I'm sick?" Or, "When I've been sick will I be able to go and have something to eat?" One minute he sounded so clever and the next he was behaving like a four year old, and reminding us of what we were trying hard to forget. To make matters worse, the middle brother returned with his father and related all the details of what they'd just eaten. We heaved.

As we neared the French coast the sun came out. Pete and I smiled to each other, remarking how we knew all along that the weather would be better once we reached Brittany. But sadly, before we could even *see* Roscoff, the sky became dark again and dampened our spirits once more.

The Spanish man amazed us by speaking to a passing acquaintance in perfect Queen's English. "Why can't he speak to his own family like that?" I hissed to Pete.

Malc appeared on the staircase and came down when he spotted us. He'd been sitting on a toilet for more than five hours, resisting the efforts of people trying to force the door open, and attempting to sleep with his head on a pipe. Amazingly, he didn't look much the worse for wear.

When the ferry docked we didn't hang about as we had the previous year - we went straight down for the bikes. They allowed us off almost immediately.

So here we were in our beloved Roscoff again, looking forward to doing all the things we'd enjoyed so much last time. I was elected to lead the way as I could remember the town better than the boys. We thought it best to buy food in town first, before finding our campsite. Then once we'd pitched the tents we could relax and not have to go out again. In our old Spa shop we stocked up with a few of our favourite items.

The campsite had altered slightly since last year. As we approached along the country road, with carrots growing in fields on either side, we noticed that wooden chalets had been built just inside the entrance gates. They were hexagonal in shape with fancy roofs and looked very avant garde. It was unsettling, seeing these rapid changes to our campsite. We wanted everything to be as it had been before.

To start the holiday in a legal manner, we went straight to the office and booked in for two nights. There were new proprietors this year. The woman taking our particulars made an awful hash of writing our address. She thought the name of the house was the town name, and the town name was the street name. We didn't enlighten her. We preferred her not knowing.

There was quite a large, vacant area in front of a bushy hedge. We'd viewed it with envy the previous year, but there hadn't been a single space for us then. Pete began to erect his tent parallel to this hedge. All the while a strong wind was blasting it at an angle, flapping the tent sides as we tried to keep the poles upright. I told him to try pitching it with the bell end into the wind. He grudgingly began following my suggestion, but that way didn't seem to work either. He yanked the pegs out again, crossly. None of us was feeling cheerful, in fact we were quite down in the dumps.

We looked around for inspiration. To our right was a neatly-clipped hedge, on the other side of which were widely-spaced caravans with lovely grass in between, mowed and perfectly flat. One or two caravans had tents pitched near to them. "Why not do likewise?" I thought.

Pete gathered his tent into a bundle and strode over the hedge. Just as he was laying the heap on the ground, an irate man rushed out from the nearest caravan and began hurling abuse at him. Pete stood shocked and bewildered, not having understood a single word, although the actions were quite explicit.

Having been on the point of stepping over the hedge myself, I made a cowardly back turn, leaving my son abandoned. Angrily, Pete snatched everything up and made for the hedge. "Non, non," screamed the man. "Allez par *là!*" He made my poor, humiliated son walk all the way round the pathway; down to the toilet block, past the office, through the opening in the hedge and up past the swings, dragging his bits and pieces behind him and steaming with fury.

What a great start to our holiday! We would have to make do with this side of the hedge after all, although we really couldn't see why we should have to. So we struggled to pitch the flapping tents in the place we'd first chosen, putting the flysheet in between to make it into one long tent with a storage place in the middle.

"Why do we have to have the opening into the field? Let's open it up on the hedge side," suggested Pete, now that he'd simmered down. "It'll be more sheltered and if we bung all our luggage along the other side we can stop the draughts. It would be better for cooking as well." It seemed like a good idea, except that we wouldn't be able to see what was going on outside.

To make it fair for the boys I was intending to sleep one night in one tent and the next in the other. That way the boys could have their tent to themselves every other night. Great for them! Well they were *their* tents. I was just the paying guest – paying for everything! The first night I was sharing with Malc.

After a late tea, mainly from tins, we nipped down for a quick look at the beach before dusk. It was bleak and uninviting, so we didn't hang about for long. With a bottle of wine and a pack of cards we might as well spend an evening indoors.

We all squeezed into Malc's tent and fixed a cycle lamp to the tent pole. For the first time I could remember, I felt claustrophobic in the tent, trapped up at the bell-end with my two growing lads blocking my exit. (In a devilish mood, they'd been known to tickle my feet, knowing full well that I'd go berserk). I played calm while we played cards and drank wine with lemonade, and pretended we were having a good time. By ten o'clock we were in our sleeping bags, listening to the wind.

* * * * *

Sudden heavy downpours startled me every time I was on the verge of sleep. It was so annoying. I thought Malc had slept through it all and I hoped Pete had, as well.

It was still showery at breakfast time and rather depressing too, especially when Pete called me into his tent to show me his big toe. I had no idea he had a problem with it. He hadn't said anything. Gently taking off his sock, he uncovered a huge red-glowing toe, twice its normal size. With agonising expressions on his face he squeezed out blood and pus. I was sickened by it.

Six months before, he had broken this toe (on a step, apparently), although I'd always suspected he was messing about doing karate kicks at the time, having just gained his 'brown belt.' Now, the new nail seemed to be growing into his toe. The sight of it tightened my stomach, even more so when I realised that I'd come without our medical insurance papers. I could remember searching for them at home without success, before completely forgetting about them.

"I'm not going to any French doctor, whatever happens," Pete stated emphatically, which rather let me off the hook, in an irresponsible sort of way. So we bathed it in a bowl of salted, warm water that I'd first boiled, then covered it with a plaster. After the pain of squeezing had worn off it didn't seem to bother him that much, and he carried on as normal.

Later that morning we decided to buy a load of new batteries for the bike lamps. Whatever fate was in store this year, we didn't want to be floundering around in the dark. We set off for the large supermarket at St Pol, but Pete refused to go via Roscoff as the roads were so full of potholes. He didn't want to risk buckling his wheels. That's when we discovered a brand new Super U just on the edge of town and only a mile from our campsite.

We bought batteries galore at bargain prices, and a tin opener as well, which was expensive. But when we tried it out later it wasn't a tin opener at all, just a multi bottle-opener. What a waste of money. Still, what the heck, the clouds were disappearing and the sun was beaming its warmth on us at last.

We changed into shorts and raced to the beach, not wanting to miss one moment of this golden rarity. Our new-found energy was boundless and we challenged each other to a mini-Olympics. Pete's toenail didn't seem to be bothering him at all now.

The first event was the long jump. The flat sand was great for take-off but made the landings painful, so we held the event in the soft stuff. I was the last to go. By the time I'd reached the jump-off line, after a thwarted run-up in soft sand, I was reduced to giggles and speechlessness. The boys named me Grandma Flump, the rotters! How could a shorty like me compete with those long pods?

We drove our legs to exhaustion; at least I did. Next we went on to the discus, which didn't make us quite so hot. It was as much a matter of how good a stone you could find as how far you could throw. Mine were spinning off at all angles.

Strewn along the margin of the high tide were great long seaweed plants, each consisting of a blackish, lumpy head, from which grew several brownish, strap-like legs. These were four feet or more in length and over an inch wide. We likened them to octopi with steam-rollered legs but named them triffids, because they were so weird. The boys grabbed one each and swung them round and round. After accidentally hitting each other once or twice, it developed into an all-out battle, which only came to an end when I suggested that they'd be good for hammer throwing. So that was our next event.

When we'd tired of that, we thought about having a dip in the sea. We tested the water. But feeling how icy the wind was on our wet legs, this idea got no further. Anyway the boys were hungry now, so we went back for tea.

By the time we were ready to resume our fun on the beach, the sky had clouded over once more, making us feel quite chilly. Disappointedly, we covered up the slight suntan we'd acquired and set off in anoraks and trousers to climb the boulders round to the next bay. As there were so many interesting things on the beach besides the triffids, we weren't bored. It was just the weather that was spoiling things. Still, if it could suddenly turn hot one day then it could do the same the next. We'd just have to be optimistic.

A bitter wind hit us as we returned to our bay. We were leaping the gaps between the boulders with me trying to keep up with the boys, although I was very conscious of the consequences if I slipped on the rough surface.

As we jumped off the last rock we almost landed on a woman out strolling along the beach, well wrapped up in a winter coat and headscarf. After her initial shock, she seemed keen to talk to us. We had a long struggling conversation with her as she waited for her husband to catch up. He was dressed like a seafaring man and, it turned out, had worked for Brittany Ferries. We told her what an awful crossing we'd had and about the even worse one the year before. By now her husband had caught up and was telling us of his experiences. We didn't really understand much of what he said, but it was a laugh trying.

Their caravan, they told us, was just beyond the first flight of steps. As darkness fell, we bade them *bonne nuit* at the bottom of the steps and made for the second flight, further along. Malc was thrilled to bits that he'd understood the odd phrase or two and hoped we'd have more chance meetings like that one.

Back in the tent, we boiled up some water to soak Pete's toe again. I hoped that as long as we kept it oozing, it would be safe. So he went through the painful squeezing ordeal once more. Malc tried to get a peep in, but had his head almost snapped off as soon as it appeared inside Pete's tent. This was a private matter. Even I would have been excluded, had it been any less serious. Afterwards, I marked the bowl with a few scratches so that I'd know which bowl *not* to wash up in.

We didn't play cards that night but just lay on our sleeping bags, reading quietly. Malc was improving his French, Pete doing crossword puzzles in his tent and I was reading my Brittany brochure, which was making me want to see so many places. Until now, we hadn't even discussed where we were going. I think the boys were leaving it up to my whims and fancies, as long as we kept near the sea.

We had a vague notion that we would travel westwards around the coast and then try to get ferried across the Rade de Brest. (We had second-hand knowledge that this was possible). Then we could pass down through the Crozon peninsula to our beloved Pentrez Plage on the Baie de Douarnenez, and from there, anywhere.

However, we weren't ready to move on yet; not while these cold and persistent north-westerly winds were blowing. Pete and Malc had brought their blow-up surfboards with them, hoping to emulate the fun they'd had last year. So far it had been out of the question. Maybe we'd have one more day here then see what the weather would do.

I read on, and got hooked on seeing Carantec, Morlaix and Thégonnec before we left the area. They were just south east of here. Perhaps tomorrow we could take a day trip. I hadn't thought of day excursions until now. It would enable us to cycle luggage-free. I tried to sell this idea to Malc, but he was only half listening and not that enthusiastic. I didn't bother Pete in his tent. He'd probably be asleep by now, anyway. Malc and I turned in for the night, more than ready for bed (I'd completely forgotten that I should be sleeping in Pete's tent tonight). A ferocious wind was blowing. I don't think I slept at all.

* * * * *

As soon as Malc woke up and rolled onto his tummy, his nose began to pour with blood. Quick as a flash, I snatched the toilet roll and flung it to him. He caught it with one hand and managed to stem the flow, without one single drop of blood spilling onto his sleeping bag. It was a marvellous feat of teamwork, we thought. What with Pete's toe and now this, we were getting through toilet rolls like nobody's business.

Pete offered to go shopping, although not at all

enthusiastically. He said he hadn't slept a wink all night because of the wind. That made two of us.

While he was gone I put various cold objects down the back of Malc's neck, which caused him to call me a few choice names. But it did the trick and eventually his nose stopped bleeding.

On Pete's return, I casually mentioned the idea of a day trip to him. But there was a distinct air of lethargy about him, which seemed to go far deeper than lack of sleep. So I gave up the idea of going anywhere at all. I'd come to the conclusion that he was plain worn out. After all the studying he'd done for his GCSEs he'd gone straight into a strenuous job, while still keeping his evening job at the Co-op. Every day he'd dashed home from work, washed, changed, gobbled his tea then jumped back on his bike and raced to the supermarket. It had all finally caught up with him, especially with the added problem of his toe. We would have a rest day.

After breakfast, I left them both reading, and took the dirty clothes up to the wash area. They still wore the blessed white socks which I *so* disliked washing. Now Pete had a yellow and red toe-stain to each pair, which meant I'd have to work even harder on them. I didn't dare let them accumulate. They would soon become smelly, even mouldy.

The previous year I'd carted a box of washing powder round in my panniers. But this year I had my revolutionary little soap tablet of Vanish. I would put it to the test.

The *lavage* area was very busy that Sunday morning. I was

amazed to see what a load of scrubbers the French were. They scrubbed everything – not just shirt collars, but pants, socks, the lot.

The sinks themselves seemed almost as deep as wells. I had to take my feet off the ground to touch the bottom (I might easily have ended up doing handstands, had I been careless).

The Vanish was adequate, but I missed having a sink full of suds and a pleasant aroma to go with it. I could only make lather at the place where I was rubbing. But as it was such a handy little tablet to carry, I was fairly happy with it.

Just beyond the sinks, a huge man was gutting four enormous fish, which he hung one at a time from the corrugated roof. They must each have been at least five feet in length. I was dying to know what sort of fish they were but he didn't look very approachable. In fact nobody looked very approachable. They were so busy. Were they going to cook a Sunday dinner after all this scrubbing?

It was already afternoon before we set off to shop for our dinner. When we reached our Super U it was closed. Oh well! We'd have to carry on to St. Pol. However, everywhere there was locked and deserted as well. This was terrible. Nowhere was open at all. We hadn't remembered that the shops closed on Sunday afternoons. Malc reminded me that there was still some hope; a snack caravan seemed to be always parked outside the campsite gates. Mostly, we tried to stay clear of such places, as they were too expensive. But if it were open, we'd just have to give in this time.

Meanwhile, the sun had appeared. We might as well stay

outside and enjoy it for a while. If we ate nearer to bedtime, we'd stand a better chance of sleeping. So we decided to hang on as long as possible.

We thought St. Pol-de-Léon must have a beach somewhere, although there was nothing very seasidey about the town. When we had a proper look, we soon found a signpost for the coast. It was barely half a mile away. As we wandered along the coastal road we chanced upon a Swiss chalet-type shop next to the beach.

When everywhere had been so deserted, it amazed us to find a multitude of men crowded around this shop counter; a convivial gathering of smokers and drinkers. To get served, we nervously squeezed through them and their smoke screen to buy cheap chocolate bars and three expensive ice creams. Then, in an obscure corner of the beach behind the shop, we sat on a low wall to savour the rare sunshine along with our treats.

Of course, as soon as the boys had finished theirs, they wanted more. I told them they'd have to use their own pocket money this time. I couldn't afford to squander any more food money today. Thanks to Grandma we each had £20 spending money, but I reminded them that if we had an emergency, we'd have to fall back on this. We had nothing else for standby. They both took the hint and refrained from going overboard. Subsequently, Pete became hooked on Hollywood gum and seemed to be incessantly chewing for days.

Before long we were bored with sitting around, so we biked off to explore the coastline, first going south towards the estuary of the river Penzé. As the narrow, twisting road climbed inland, we looked behind us to see a beautiful view of Carantec across the bay. Conveniently, there was a wooden bench by the roadside near the top. I was gasping by now. We stopped to drink our water as we gazed down on the panorama that had unfolded with the climb. Pity we didn't have the camera with us. Anyway we weren't sure if it worked. Jim had bought it for 50p in a car-boot sale and so far, we hadn't used it. Well, at least I'd *seen* Carantec. That was one off my list.

Just lately, I had seemed to be always lagging behind the boys, partly because my bike was older and heavier than theirs, and probably because my body was older and heavier than theirs too! But all things considered, my bike was being uncooperative. It was giving me a hard time. I would have to check it over when I got back.

We could smell the vapours coming from the snack caravan even before it came into view, so we knew it was still open. What a relief. But it had been quite stupid of us to leave it this late. The place could easily have been locked up by now.

Each of us spent F10 from the food money. Pete and Malc had large portions of chips, while I chose a ham baguette. But so determined was I to get some sleep that I paid F20 for a bottle of wine. It was the cheapest one they had, and I intended to share it. The boys gave me very disapproving looks. What was all this stuff I'd been saying about being careful with our money?

Approaching the tents, while hungrily scoffing food from one hand and trying to push our bikes with the other, we were alarmed by a sudden rush of wings from under our flysheet. A flock of squawking sparrows disappeared into the hedge. What the heck was going on? Was this a regular happening?

I looked at the hedge and realised what an unwholesome place it was to have my kitchen next to. No doubt everyone threw slops and scraps into it. And apart from housing a very cheerful and abundant flock of sparrows, it was probably home to equally happy rats and mice. I would have to be on my guard.

Over a cup of tea we discussed our various bike problems. When I went to spin my back wheel it stopped after barely three revolutions, which worried me no end. I assumed it would need a new axle or ball bearings in the middle. Pete was equally worried about his bottom bracket because his pedals kept creaking. He thought it needed tightening with a specialised tool; the one he'd forgotten to bring. Tomorrow morning we must find the Roscoff cycle shop and see if they could sort everything out for us.

I began to wonder if we'd ever leave this place at all, what with the unpredictable weather and now the bikes. The prospect was becoming scary. We were safe while we were only a few miles from the ferry, but once we sallied forth, that was it. We'd have to cope with whatever transpired. I was beginning not to trust our bikes.

However, we put our worries aside, finished our tea and went off boulder bounding to the next bay. The evening was fine, so we might as well enjoy it.

At the end of a little lane, which petered out into the sand, we found a rusty length of heavy metal with a slightly knobbly surface. We presumed it had once been the tailboard of a lorry. It made an ideal running board for our long jump. Now we could have a firm run up with a soft landing. So we had a fairly serious competition this time. Malc was quite amazed at my ability. He found that I wasn't that bad at it, after all. In fact I wasn't much more than a foot behind him. But Pete was always a squeak in front, in spite of his toe.

A lady came down the lane walking her dog. She gave me a really funny look. I suppose she thought I was crackers, but I didn't care. I was engrossed in my long jump and quite pleased with myself.

The sun was sinking behind some isolated rocks, making an impressive scene full of textures. I longed to take some artistic photos. But the boys didn't volunteer to fetch the camera for me or offer to stay there if I dashed back for it myself, so we just walked back together. By the time we'd reached the tents it was too late anyway. The glow had gone and the colour was dissipating from everything. These moments don't last. Maybe tomorrow I'd get a chance.

After a swig or two of wine (I had two beakers full, although it was like paint stripper) we dropped into bed. But sleep evaded me, for around midnight a gang of young men came parading through the campsite. They were shouting and making a hell of a commotion yet somehow, at the same time, singing *Frère Jacques* in an endless round.

I worried about what they would do to our bikes if they saw

them, locked in a triangle outside on the grass. Perhaps they'd fall over them. At the same time I was fascinated to hear Frenchmen singing their own song as, until now, I'd only ever heard it sung by English schoolgirls. It sounded quite beautiful. My feelings alternated between panic and relief, as the sound came nearer then faded away again.

By the time they had left the site for good, still singing and with their arms linked together (I'd been out to have a look), I was wide-awake and listening to the wind again. I didn't know if the boys were awake or not. I didn't ask in case I woke them up.

* * * * *

There was still no significant change in the weather except that the wind had dropped. It was we who would have to change our outlook.

While we ate our Weetabix, we came to terms with the fact that the way things were looking, this was unlikely to be a swimming and sunbathing holiday. So what could we do? Well we could visit more places and take lots of pictures. At least then we'd have *something* to look back on. If we each put £3 of our pocket money into the kitty we could buy a new camera. That way we'd be sure of our photos coming out ok.

"Let's buy a radio as well," suggested Pete, "then we'll have something to listen to when the weather's bad." That seemed like a reasonable idea. Perhaps we could take the cost of that out of our food money.

At the beginning of this holiday, allowing twenty days as

the maximum we could stay (and we knew we'd try to, just to get our money's worth on the ferry fare), we had £17 per day for food and camping. Now, and only four days into the holiday, that average was already down to £15. Even so, I reckoned we could afford a cheap radio. However we mustn't forget the bikes. What would they cost to repair?

I took the cycle oil out to my bike and squeezed the nozzle onto the back axle at every angle possible. Then I spun the wheel – and it spun beautifully. I felt such an ass. I'd thought it would need major surgery when just a drop of oil had cured it. Hadn't I oiled everything before we'd left home? Obviously not. But at least that was one problem less. We'd better get off to Roscoff now and sort out Pete's bike.

With Pete leading the way and Malc and me following like sheep, we somehow ended up at the Super U first, to buy the radio. It was obvious that Pete's priorities had shifted today!

We were lucky. They had a demonstration radio, complete with batteries, for only F60. It had a slight fault, in that the lid holding the batteries in place wouldn't stay shut, but we could remedy that easily with a bit of sticky tape. It was a very neat little thing.

Right. Now we *must* sort out Pete's bottom bracket. This time I led the way, because Pete didn't know where to find the shop. I remembered it as being more like a garage than a shop. We found it in a back street, with its doors wide open and everyone very busy in there. So busy in fact, that we couldn't attract anyone's attention at all. We parked our bikes against the wall and noticed that they now had a brand new double-fronted cycle shop joined onto the back of the garage.

We browsed in the windows for a while but soon realised we were getting in the way of pedestrians, who were forced to walk in the road. It might be better to go inside for a look. It *was* better. We were served as soon as the doorbell rang.

Pete's bike was taken into the garage straight away, but they couldn't find anything wrong with it. So with Pete's mind now at rest, he didn't mention it any more. Having been prepared to spend *some* money, we felt we couldn't leave without buying something, especially as we hadn't been charged for the diagnosis. Pete was attracted to a blue-and-white striped seat cover (in fact he was attracted by everything). I bought a bike lock from a sale basket. I thought it might be handy to have a spare one, although it was a sickly purple colour. Malc was sensible and bought nothing.

That was the bike problems sorted. Now we needed a camera. We thought St. Pol would be the best place to buy it, but when we arrived the shops were just closing for lunch. What a nuisance. We'd have to hang around for more than two hours.

We plodded the streets, studying the contents of every single shop window, even if we weren't particularly interested. When we'd done the whole of the main street and one or two side streets as well, we thought we'd explore the outskirts on the other side of town.

Malc and I had wanted to go up the Chapel de Kreisker in the middle of the town with its 169 steps. From the top, on a clear day, it is possible to see the Ile de Batz to the north and the Arrée mountains to the south, (so I'd read). But it was closed. That pleased Pete, because he wasn't really interested right now. I'd managed to kindle a bit of enthusiasm in Malc, by encouraging him to read snippets from my Brittany booklet.

The other side of St. Pol was quite drab at first with a railway crossing next to a few dowdy sheds that looked like abattoirs. Beyond these however, were neat little roads, where the modern houses had well-kept little front gardens. Not very different from suburbia in England, I thought. It was easy to imagine that we weren't even in France.

We wandered further than we need have done, then felt annoyed that we had so far to ride back into town. The shops would have reopened already. We made straight for the camera shop. We'd already sussed it out. After a fairly brief look at the cheaper range we chose a compact one for less than F100. We realised we'd need a film as well, so I paid for that out of the food money.

After that I would have liked to return to the spot we'd cycled to yesterday, as I so wanted to take a photo of Carantec from across the bay. But it wasn't sunny as it had been then, and anyway we had to buy food from somewhere and cart it back to the campsite.

While I was browsing postcards outside a newsagent's, I spotted an English newspaper. Just what we needed! We could read tomorrow's weather forecast. I decided to buy a French paper as well, just to be intellectual. But when I'd paid for them plus three postcards, I found I'd been short-changed. I dilly-dallied about in the back of the shop for a while before plucking up courage to challenge the shopkeeper. If he started gabbling on I'd be lost. Oh well!

I went back to the counter. He totted it up again and the amount was the same as before. I walked away, flummoxed but not satisfied. After a moment's hesitation I went back and challenged him a second time. Again he added it up but more slowly this time. Still it came to the same amount. Then the penny dropped. I realised that the English paper was almost four times as much as the French one. I apologised to him, feeling such an idiot. If I'd had the guts I would have returned the paper and asked to have my money back, especially as I'd already found the weather forecast inside. It was no good to us at all. All it showed were the temperatures around the world.

For someone who was supposed to be good at managing on very little money, with years of experience (equivalent to degree level, I sometimes thought) I was being very lax indeed. If I didn't get my act together soon, we'd only afford half a holiday. So why was I looking at all these souvenirs, wondering what I could take back to my friends and relatives? I'd better remove myself from the temptation.

We pedalled off to find the Rallye Supermarché we'd frequented last year. It didn't look familiar, approached from the opposite direction, but inside it was just the same. We bought some tinned stuff for tea; nothing elaborate. I didn't feel like putting much effort into it. I spotted suntan lotion on a shelf which was identical to the one I'd bought in England but half the price.

Our tummies were rumbling by now. We'd been out all day

and since breakfast time had eaten nothing more than a bit of chocolate and an apple each. No wonder we all felt quite gloomy.

Even after eating we weren't much more cheerful. The weather was *so* drab. We'd hung around here for almost four days now and seemed to have lost all incentive to move on. Last year we'd had Tom with us. He had been a pain in the neck at times but he'd made us laugh. I think we were missing him now. Pete was pretty serious with just family, and Malc was desperately trying to fill the humour gap left by Tom.

I went for a walk with Malc. Pete didn't want to join us - he had the radio now - and took our usual route over the boulders. It was a challenge we enjoyed, but I wondered how long I'd get away with climbing in these loose shoes before I slipped, like last year. But I was being reasonably careful.

Beyond the next headland was another bay, totally different. A clump of evergreen trees stood tall from the centre of a castle-like keep, which jutted out towards the sea. Its overall shape was rather like a keyhole. It was built of stone on a rocky outcrop with a ramp leading up to a huge locked doorway.

By climbing on to nearby rocks, we could step across to reach a narrow ledge, which was halfway up the wall. This ledge went all the way round the outside. It wasn't a difficult feat - anyone could have done it. There were places where we could almost have climbed over into the castle grounds, but we didn't try. There were dogs barking inside. I presumed that when this castle was first built it would have been surrounded by water. Now it was left high and dry and accessible. Conversely, it might just be a folly like the one near us back home.

We'd cheered up considerably by the time we'd finished our little jaunt. Things weren't so bad after all.

Coming back along the beach I found tiny shells of different colours and patterns. Malc helped me to gather some. They were really pretty.

When we looked up, Pete was coming towards us across the shingle. We hadn't expected him. He was in one of those 'don't really want to do anything' sort of moods. However, we had an unenthusiastic game of boules using big pebbles, then climbed the high rocks back to our 'tailboard' bay. We attempted a few half-hearted long jumps, but by the time we'd finished, our spirits were all dragged down to the level of Pete's doldrums again. Tomorrow we would be moving on. We had no more excuses to stay. But we didn't know where we were going, or why.

After tidying-up a bit to make packing easier in the morning, we drank the rest of yesterday's wine, but with plenty of lemonade to sweeten it.

Pete went into his tent to do his toe. If anything, it seemed a bit worse, but he'd only allowed me a brief peep that morning. Now he wouldn't let me look at it at all.

This was our fourth night and still I was sleeping in Malc's tent. I promised him I'd spend the next four nights in Pete's tent. It seemed too much effort to uproot myself, and my belongings, every single night.

I opened my Brittany book for inspiration and was duly inspired. "What's the point of going right round the coast if it's too cold to swim?" I said. "Why don't we cut straight across the middle to the south coast and see if the weather's better there?"

I don't know why we hadn't thought of that before. Anticipating this new idea made us feel slightly excited and a teeny bit adventurous. It also gave us hope. Surely, even with north-westerly winds blowing, it would be warmer down there.

We finished our drink, snacked on a few odds and ends that needed eating up and turned in for the night, cheerfully.

Perhaps I dropped off to sleep for a while but it couldn't have been for long. There was too much noise coming from outside – shouting and music. I crawled out to have a look. I thought so! It was that crowd who'd arrived earlier and put up a large tent close to ours. It had an awning as big as a dining room and they'd begun their evening meal *after* we'd gone to bed. There were loads of them, mums, dads and kids, all seated on chairs at a big table. They hadn't acknowledged us at all, or any other campers for that matter. No one else seemed to matter to them, such was their selfishness. Just the noise of their knives and forks clicking and clacking was enough to drive anyone to distraction.

I listened to Malc. He was blissfully asleep. For me, it was going to be more wine and less lemonade in the future. I looked up into the darkness. "God, are you ever going to let me get some sleep?" I pleaded. But the party continued until 3 am.

Heading south

St Pol-de-Léon, Huelgoat, Quimperlé, Carnac

Although we tried to be efficient, nothing seemed to fit in, now that we'd used it. We still had two and a half boxes of Weetabix left, so there was hardly any extra space in the panniers. But Pete made room for the radio without any fuss and I took the new camera and some left-over crisps. Malc squeezed half a packet of biscuits into his front bag. We still had an unopened packet of rusks. They were such an awkward shape that we couldn't fit them in anywhere. So I discreetly placed them in front of a couple's small tent as we were passing, hoping they'd get eaten.

It was already midday. The sun had come out, which cheered us up no end. This was it. I couldn't wait to get going. We were finally setting off on holiday, hoping that the toe, the bikes and the weather would all behave themselves.

Wishful thinking! Barely halfway to St. Pol, Pete pulled into a layby and began fiddling with his front wheel. When I caught up and saw the grim expression on his face, my heart sank.

"Should we be making this journey at all?" I thought, as he then took off his roll and panniers and turned the bike upside down.

After a tense quarter of an hour with neither Malc nor me daring to say a word, Pete was ready to move on. We never did understand what the problem was. Pete was muttering under his breath and I couldn't be bothered to keep saying "pardon." All I knew was that he had been hoping for utter perfection in his newly equipped Raleigh Equipe bike. He'd spent so much time and money on it. But, whatever minor fault it had, he'd hopefully decided to live with it.

As we rode through the centre of St. Pol the market was in full swing. Seeing the tempting fruit stalls, we realised we were peckish. "Better eat now," I suggested. "It's past lunch time." Inside though, I was cringing at the amount of time we were wasting. So much for our early start!

We bought bananas, apples and a baguette, hoping to devour them as quickly as possible. But in this bustling market place there was absolutely nowhere to put the bikes, and our hands were now full. The only space available was behind a buttress of the cathedral. We parked the bikes there and squatted in front of them to gobble our lunch.

Across the road I could discern several pairs of eyes staring out at us from the dark doorway of a gloomy bar, although I couldn't make out the faces. I felt like sticking my tongue out. "No, mustn't let the British down," I thought. According to my upbringing, I shouldn't even be eating in the street!

At last, after traipsing around the cathedral to look for a loo, we were ready to move on. 2 pm already and we'd only ridden three miles. But now it *really* felt as if we were starting our holiday. All that time we'd spent in Roscoff when we could have been heading south to warmer weather!

We followed the main road as far as the river Penzé, where we swooped down, then up and over a bridge. The ground levelled out as we branched off the main road. I noticed that Carantec was across the bay behind us. I asked the boys if they'd pose for a photo in front of the view, though Carantec was too far away to be recognisable. They willingly obliged. We had to make use of our new camera.

Further on we crossed a slow moving river, which had a serene, Constable look about it. Before long we had rounded a bend to find ourselves on the beautiful Rade de Morlaix. The road was cut into the rock and snaked along, following the course of the river exactly. Pete and Malc were sailing along with gusto, leaving me struggling to match their pace. The sun was shining brightly now. I'd forced myself to keep up with them for far too long and now I suddenly came over all light-headed.

"I shall have to stop and eat something," I shouted to the boys. They didn't hear. "HANG ON!" I shouted a bit louder, and as I did so, we came to a picnic area cut into the rocks. "How's that for timing!" I thought.

With relief, I flopped down at a picnic table. What a piddling ration of food we had to share; a few crisps, three biscuits and an apple each. I felt a need for some sugar, so went over to my bike to fetch some. But what I found was a strong smell of gas with an ominous hiss coming from one of the panniers. Blast! The gas canister was leaking, and I'd only bought it that morning. I must have knocked the tap on while I was packing. Damn! I'd have to buy another one tonight. It could be almost empty now.

There were two English vehicles in the picnic area. A family of four in a red car smiled faintly at us, whereas a couple in a Volkswagen camper van positively scowled. "Be like that," muttered Pete under his breath. "Let's get moving."

"Hey, Mum's bike seat's got measles," exclaimed the boys as I went to cock my leg over. It was covered with big white spots. We all burst out laughing when we realised they were transfers from my new spotty trousers. "Stuff the camper van couple" I thought as I plonked my spotty bottom down on the saddle. "Who needs a smile from them?"

We continued along the water's edge, enjoying the scenery. Occasionally we'd see a small sailing ship moored near the bank. As we got closer to Morlaix the density of boats increased until, by the end of the navigable river they were choc-a-bloc, with their rigging jingling in the wind.

Morlaix was an impressive sight. A huge viaduct spanned the valley, dominating the entrance to the town. We'd never seen anything like this before. Time for a photo!

We spent ages wandering the streets, quite fascinated by the buildings and the topography and feeling almost as proper tourists ought to. If the cafés had still been serving lunches we might have had a meal, but they weren't, so I bought a couple of postcards instead.

In the dank shadows of the viaduct we found some absolutely disgusting toilets. I had to cover my nose *and* eyes

Malc and me, keen to be photographed with the impressive viaduct at Morlaix

as I passed the open doorway of the men's toilet to reach the dark inner vestry that served as 'les femmes'. But needs must! As I emerged into daylight I almost collided with a lady who was coming in. I apologised in English because her Esso Tiger T-shirt was a giveaway. My uncle sold them in his Esso garage back home.

We left Morlaix on the D769 towards Huelgoat, having pushed our bikes all the way to the top of town. It was a scenic route, often wild and wooded with foxgloves growing in the verges. But it was uphill all the way. Malc was out in front, while I was struggling to keep up. The boys were constantly stopping to wait for me.

In the middle of nowhere we came unexpectedly across a small roadside shop, which gave us a nice break from our cycling. It sold a vast variety of loose sweets, so we bought loads of them. But we annoyed the shopkeeper by paying with all our small change. When Malc went back for more sweets she asked if he still had his paper bag. He was offended that she hadn't offered him a fresh one, but pleased because he'd understood what she'd said.

It was 6.30 pm when we reached Huelgoat. On the verge, next to the place name, was a large board showing a map of the town. We searched it and found a campsite by a lake. Our immediate thoughts were that it would be too expensive for us. But we were surprised to find it was only F35 (about £3.50) per night. That was ok. Then I remembered; I'd forgotten to pay for the extra two nights that I owed in Roscoff. Too late now!

While the boys put up the tents I cycled back to a supermarket we'd seen just out of town. The sky was black and menacing. I expected to get a soaking at any moment. But it didn't rain at all.

There wasn't any gas for sale in the supermarket, so I wasn't sure how I would cook dinner. Three English boys, who were busy putting up their tent the other side of the hedge, heard us discussing our dilemma. They looked over and asked if we'd like to borrow their paraffin cooker. I gladly accepted. One of them began walking all the way round to bring it to me. It was quite a trek. Meanwhile, an Englishman who'd just stepped out of his car told us he had a spare canister just like ours and sold it to us.

The boy arrived carrying the paraffin cooker, smiling all over his face. I felt so mean having to tell him that I'd just bought some gas. Fortunately he didn't show any animosity. He just turned tail and trotted all the way back. But I was glad the hedge was taller than me. I could keep a low profile.

We had big omelettes with crisps and tomatoes for our dinner. Surprisingly, the original gas lasted until I'd nearly finished cooking. After having coffee and chatting with the boys over the hedge (who were also cycling) we decided to turn in for the night. As promised, I was now in Pete's tent.

All was blissfully quiet until the couple from next door came back late and slammed their car doors, loudly. Then it was ZZiiiiip as they opened their tent forcefully and ZZiiiiip as they closed it, with equal disregard for the rest of us. Next it was ZZiiiip, ZZiiiiip as they zipped up their sleeping bags with great vigour. Several minutes of silence followed. Then we heard ZZiiiiip, as one got up, ZZiiiiip as they opened the tent at great speed (presumably to go to the toilet block) and ZZiiiiip to close it hastily behind them. We hung on. When the inconsiderate so-and-so had returned and was safely zipped into the tent, we waited patiently for the last, loud ZZiiiiip of their sleeping bag. At last! They were settled in for the night.

We sighed with relief. But more was to follow, for minutes later the other one got up and we had to endure the whole performance all over again. We were zipping mad by the time they'd settled down.

* * * * *

The next morning was a fine one to wake up to, even if the sun was rather milky. Our intention was to make an early start. I managed to drag myself from the warmth of my sleeping bag without too much effort. I wanted to have a shower and they were free.

This campsite was very well appointed and set in a pretty, wooded area next to a lake. This was probably why it attracted so many English families. It wasn't surprising to walk into the showers and imagine you were in England. There wasn't a foreign voice to be heard. "Not really what we've come to France for," I thought. But my shower was long enough and hot enough and when it finally ran cold, I forced myself to stand under it, just to be further invigorated.

We ate a swift breakfast of Weetabix and gathered our

belongings together. Then we set about packing, without speaking a word. This wasn't as a result of falling out with each other or of being in a bad mood but because we were working efficiently. It was really good teamwork. We were ready to leave by 9.30 am. The boys on the other side of the hedge beat us by half an hour. We shouted "Cheerio" to them as they headed north, for home.

Luckily I'd found time to look up Huelgoat in my Brittany booklet. Apparently, just across the road from us was a grotto in the forest. In it we would find fascinating rock shapes with names like the Devil's Grotto with its underground stream, the Virgin's Kitchen, (a pile of boulders in the shape of kitchen utensils), Mill Rock, Mill Rock Chaos and the Trembling Rock. "Let's get going!" we exclaimed.

We were enraptured by this grotto, clambering over enormous boulders, peering down fathomless ravines and trying to work out which kitchen utensils were which. It didn't really matter that it had started raining and we needed to put anoraks on, except that the moss had become slippery, so we were extra careful crossing the gaps.

After numerous photo-shots and explorations to the end of the valley, we dragged ourselves away. It was almost midday.

There weren't any main roads leading south, in fact there were no significant ones at all. We found ourselves on what were more like tracks, although they were metalled, to a degree. The going was tough and the weather showery with a light wind, but it wasn't cold or unpleasant. I found myself steaming hot in my old anorak. It didn't allow me much

With Pete on the more accessible boulders in the Grotto at Huelgoat

breathing space. Pete called me a 'portable sauna'. With the camera in my front pocket and the way my anorak puffed up in the wind, I think I looked pregnant more than anything!

According to the map, we were crossing les Montagnes Noires, which weren't mountains at all, just loads and loads of lumpy hills. But we'd reached a slightly smoother road by now and were heading south-east towards the little town of Gourin.

Unfortunately, I reached Gourin quicker than expected. I rode straight out onto the main road. Luckily for me, the road was very quiet. We realised we hadn't seen a single vehicle or person since leaving Huelgoat. Having enjoyed this isolation, we didn't tarry in Gourin, but continued straight through to the other side of town, still going south and following Pete down another narrow road. He had the map.

We could see these little roads on our map, although we couldn't pinpoint exactly where we were. But now it did feel as if we were on farm tracks, being bumped and shaken all over the place.

As I rode over a really rough bit on the brow of a hill, there was a sudden crunch and my front wheel stopped dead. I hung on and looked down to see that my front light was smashed in the wheel. That would teach me a lesson! Hadn't I been told not to fix a front light onto tapering forks? It was bound to slip down into the wheel. I thought I'd got away with it by wrapping a thick layer of rubber round the forks first, before clamping the lamp holder on, very tightly. What if I'd been careering downhill? I felt very contrite as I picked up the pieces while Pete unscrewed the fitting, which was now dangling from the frame.

We carried on. But minutes later Pete heard a cracking noise. He was horrified to find his pannier rack had snapped on one side, leaving his roll and panniers lopsided and unsupported. Whatever were we going to do now? We were in the middle of nowhere. It was extremely disconcerting. Perhaps we should find our way back to Gourin?

But Pete, ever the innovator, soon had the answer. He strapped a flat spanner vertically across the break with loads of insulation tape, then stuck a screwdriver horizontally across the spanner. Using loads more insulation tape he attached this to the back fork of the bike frame. He made a really good job of it. Now we could carry on, with caution.

Gingerly, we continued until we came to the next village, Le Saint. We searched the handful of shops on the sloping street, looking for a garage. But it was the pâtisserie that caught our eye first. We couldn't resist. I went in for three *pains au raisins*. We'd only had a banana each since breakfast-time.

There wasn't a garage to be seen anywhere, only a lawnmower shop which also had two heavy bikes for sale. As we peered into the window, two little brown dogs came racing round the corner, yapping and snarling. They chased us down the street away from the shop front. But realising that this shop might be our only hope, we challenged them and using our bikes as shields, we made our way back up the street.

Safely inside the premises, we asked the lady if they had a pannier rack for sale. We stood about awkwardly, waiting ages and ages in silence for her to reply. (Her brain was probably working out what we'd asked for – VERY slowly). "Non" was the eventual answer.

Could they repair it, perhaps? The lady came out to see what the problem was then led us up a little lane by the side of the shop. Round at the back they had a garage-cum-workshop plus the two little brown dogs! These two monsters were licking us now. We gave them bits of cake.

The husband was in the workshop wearing clogs. Pete took the luggage off the rack and showed him where it was broken. The two pannier-rack supports were flat-sectioned metal with three holes in each, for adjusting the height. That's where the weakness was. The metal had snapped right across a hole.

With some sharp cutters, the man clipped off the broken end and attached a piece of Meccano-like metal in its place with nuts and bolts. Not content with mending it, he went round all the nuts and bolts, graunching them up with brute force. Then he bent over the rack, trying to straighten it with forceful thrusts. Pete and I looked at each other in alarm. He would break the other side, the way he was going.

We leaned over to see that there was indeed a crack in the other support. But he told us it was only in the chrome. To prove it, he scratched the chrome off. He was very domineering.

The lady said she was going to fetch her tiny book. We didn't know what she meant, but she returned with a little French–English dictionary. It *was* tiny, about 2" x 1½". It wasn't very useful to her. The print was *so* small she could barely see which letter of the alphabet she was on. But she managed to get a few words out of it.

They asked Pete my age. I felt quite cross with him because he added on a couple of years. The man kicked his leg out behind him and said that I'd got a lot of kick in me yet! We laughed. They kept finding things to say and didn't seem to want us to leave. They were obviously enjoying our company.

We happened to convey to them that the boys' panniers didn't hang very low on the racks. With that, the man clomped over to Malc's bike and bent over it, spanner in hand. He began to undo the nuts and bolts to lower the rack. We tapped him urgently on the shoulder and shouted, "Non, non" and tried to explain that they were really *front* panniers. *That* was why they didn't hang down so low.

He didn't understand. We repeated this explanation to the lady but meanwhile he was leaning over the bike to have another go. Twice more we had to stop him because as soon as we turned to tell the lady what we meant, he was back on the job.

We managed to stop him eventually, but gave up trying to explain. By now our brains were almost as tired as our legs. But all in all, it had been quite a pleasant distraction and he only charged us 50c.

From Le Saint we rode towards the main road, having had enough of farm tracks for one day. We were gutted to see a signpost for Gourin reading '8K'. All those bumpy, extra miles we'd ridden and the consequences they'd caused! Now, apart from one or two steep hills the rest of the ride was much easier. We rolled along nicely for several miles until we came to a smaller road leading to Quimperlé. There was hardly any traffic and the evening sun shone brightly as we arrived.

The campsite looked more like a municipal park with its short, mown grass and neat edges and was adjacent to a football ground. Pete and Malc wasted no time putting up the tents while I found a supermarket nearby. It would be dark quite soon. While I was cooking our fish fingers and eggs, the neon lights lit up all around us.

I was in Pete's tent again. It was a different kettle of fish in here. There was none of the light-hearted banter Malc and I enjoyed. Pete seemed quite serious these days but I suspected that he was trying to act all grown up and responsible, so much so that sometimes it seemed as if he were *my* parent. If only Tom had been around with his witty comments and silly jokes, Pete might have loosened up a bit. Being a sibling, Malc couldn't fill the humour gap left by Tom.

Perhaps the underlying cause of all this seriousness was to do with his toe. He'd been fastidiously soaking it in salt water twice a day and had no doubt been squeezing it as well. Now I was privileged to see what state it was in. It looked just as inflamed and swollen as before, but maybe it wasn't pus that was oozing from it but just plasma. It might be better if he stopped the squeezing. The nail might chase its own course if we left it alone.

When it had been dried and covered with cotton wool and a plaster, we crawled into our sleeping bags for a well-deserved sleep. It was extremely quiet. But as the lights stayed on all night, I found it quite difficult to drop off to sleep.

* * * * *

The next morning, Pete and I took down the tents while Malc went shopping for a few essentials. He returned with a pack of SIX toilet rolls. That was the smallest amount they sold at the supermarket, so I couldn't chastise him.

Over breakfast we'd studied the map and decided to go to Carnac, way down along the south coast of Brittany, towards Vannes. According to our booklet, the area is famous the world over for its prehistoric stone alignments. We would find hundreds and hundreds of standing stones there, called 'menhirs' in Breton.

It was quite a fresh, bright morning when we left Quimperlé. We were full of enthusiasm as we sped eastwards along a main road, racing up moderate hills in top gear. My energy felt boundless. I wasn't impeded by the 'six-pack,' which was strapped on top of my red roll and sticking into my back.

The dark forests fell away to our right and towered over us on the left. We felt exhilarated, swooping up hill and down dale all the way to Pont Scorff, where we continued without stopping until we reached the walled town of Hennebont. Here we admired the ancient walls as we rode into the town, but we only stopped long enough for light refreshments before setting off again. This was a cycling day. We just wanted to get on with it.

Now we were heading south on a lesser road in gently undulating countryside. In the morning we hadn't encountered much traffic at all. There was even less here.

After several miles we came to a small river estuary with

Pete pitching his tent on the municipal site in Quimperlé

Among the menhirs – Pete caught on camera

boats lying stranded on the muddy banks. We pedalled alongside it for a while to where it reached a much wider inlet. Ahead, we could see a long, flat bridge spanning a vast expanse of water. It was a pleasant view but we didn't stop to take photos. We were enjoying our cycling too much.

In Brittany a lot of place names start with the letter K. There were plenty of examples here. Before the bridge we passed through Kerros and Kergouric, then continued on the other side through Kergo and Kerdonnerch.

Soon we were on the long, straight Rue des Menhirs. Nearly there! When we saw the masses of standing stones we were overwhelmed. There were rows and rows of them; acres and acres, everywhere we looked. Now we did get the cameras out.

We spent ages wandering through these menhirs, absolutely fascinated by the alignments, wondering what their true purpose had been. Eventually we realised that time was getting away with us. We still had to look for a campsite.

There were no camping signs at all in the town of Carnac. We carried on through to Carnac Plage, which was a completely separate place. It was brimming with people. The campsite, when we found it, was choc-a-bloc with tents. We scoured the whole site in vain and couldn't find a space anywhere. Then we saw more tents in a nearby field. Following the hedgerow around the perimeter we reached a gateway and pushed the bikes through. This would do. At least the ground was dry.

We had to trample down the long grass in order to pitch

the tents. It was tough and straw-like but would make a springy base for sleeping on.

We all helped to put up the tents, then lounged outside to enjoy a well deserved rest in the late afternoon sunshine. Many of our fellow campers greeted us. They seemed a friendly bunch. What a difference from last night in Quimperlé, where we hadn't spoken to a soul. They explained why the campsite was so full - it was the windsurfing championships fortnight.

A red Renault car came creeping through the gate, driven by an elderly lady with a large white poodle sitting next to her in the passenger seat. We watched as both the woman and the dog looked from left to right in unison as the car made slow progress around the field. We laughed our heads off. It was so funny. However, when it stopped outside our tent we were taken aback. Did she know us? Well no, but she certainly knew *of* us. We hadn't booked in and she was the proprietress.

This wasn't a deliberate ploy on our part. We hadn't thought of this field as being part of the campsite. We'd assumed that because of its rough state, it would be free. She gave me a lift back to the office, where I paid for two nights.

One of the windsurfers asked if we'd like to go over to his tent for a drink after supper. We said we would. Malc and I found some shops, where we bought a bottle of wine to share with him, as well as some raspberry syrup and a large tin of ravioli with chicken in it for our dinner. The chicken ravioli was revolting, but we managed to swallow it down with the help of the raspberry syrup.

When I'd washed up we went over for a convivial evening

of wine and conversation with our new acquaintance. But once we'd exhausted our limited vocabulary, it became quite a struggle to think of new things to talk about. So feeling more strained than relaxed, we bade him goodnight, wishing him luck for his competition the next day.

The sun was setting. I thought there might just be time to phone Jim before dark, as so far I'd only sent a postcard to say we'd arrived safely. Now I was feeling a bit guilty about it. There must be a phone box in the vicinity. Pete said he'd help me to find one. As Malc was more than ready to get to bed, we left him behind.

Darkness was approaching more quickly than we'd anticipated. We really ought to have brought a torch with us. But we wouldn't be long.

The sudden ring of a bike bell startled us as we stepped out into the road. We jumped hastily aside to avoid being mown down. A strange apparition was heading our way. And what an incredible sight it was; an EIGHT SEATER bike! We could hardly believe our eyes. We waved to the eight jovial cyclists as they rode by in a long line, hoping they'd manage to negotiate the corner ahead of them. Were they from a circus, perhaps? We walked on towards town in high spirits.

Then a plaintive noise coming from a ditch stopped us in our tracks. We peered over to see a cat lying there, crying out in pain. Its fur was matted with blood. This sight changed our mood instantly. We felt helpless. What could we do? It was no doubt somebody's beloved pet and we must try to find its owner. There were a few houses further up the road on the other side. That's probably where it had come from.

With a feeling of great urgency we groped our way up each garden path in turn, brushing by bushes and tripping up steps in the gathering darkness. We knocked on every front door but none was answered. What a hopeless situation this was proving to be. Now all we could do was keep heading towards Carnac and hope we'd find someone, very soon, whom we could inform.

On the outskirts of town was a block of four telephone boxes. Should we phone now, or try to get help for the cat first? We didn't have to make that choice because a brief investigation proved three kiosks to be card operated and the fourth to be out of order. We rushed on into town, where we could hear English people talking all over the place.

One of a group was talking in fluent French to a couple outside a restaurant. We interrupted the conversation to tell him about the cat and its whereabouts. Hopefully he'd pass this information on to local residents. What more could we do? We lessened our pace and continued searching for a telephone box although, by now, I didn't feel much like ringing home. But since we'd set out to phone Jim and had trekked so far, we were reluctant to give up.

At last we saw a couple of kiosks in the town centre. They looked brand new. As we struggled to understand the operating instructions, a young woman with long, red hair accosted us. In a soft Irish voice she explained what we had to do, then left us to it. We spent ages trying to follow her instructions but we hadn't been listening properly, such was our anxious state. In the end we gave up. What a fiasco!

Our walk back was lit slightly by the rising moon. We checked the ditch and found that the cat had gone. Had it been rescued? We sincerely hoped so and trusted that its wounds were being tended to, right now. Then at least our excursion would not have been in vain.

As we made our way back across the field we were horrified to see a shadowy figure lurking outside our tent. It filled us with dread. Malc was in there, all alone and fast asleep. We ran towards the tent, stumbling over long grass, weak at the knees. Then we realised that the figure *was* Malc. Poor lad, he was almost sick with worry. "Where've you been?" He blubbed. "It's ten to midnight. I thought something bad had happened to you." I hadn't realised how late it was and felt truly ashamed for leaving him so long. After all, he was more precious to me than an injured cat *or* a phone call home, and we *were* in a foreign land.

* * * * *

The next morning, another dull day greeted us. The boys couldn't get motivated. Pete lay on his sleeping bag doing endless crossword puzzles, while Malc moped about outside, watching the planes flying low overhead. They were probably landing at nearby Lorient airport.

The arrival of a bread van brightened our morning. We hadn't expected one to come to *our* field. Malc went over to buy some baguettes. There and then we ripped one apart. It was so crusty and warm. It didn't matter that we had nothing to put on it or in it.

After that pleasant interlude we felt a bit livelier. The dirty clothes were piling up, including ten more pairs of the dreaded white socks. I thought I should do some washing, after all there was a good wind blowing and it wasn't raining as yet. Pete offered to put up a couple of clothes lines for me, glad to have something to do.

The *lavage* area was on the edge of the proper campsite; just a row of four deep sinks with a cantilevered roof over, rather like a bus shelter. In the hot water I worked up a meagre lather with my little tablet of Vanish, tackling my own underwear first. Glancing up, I saw that a tall, dark and very handsome young man was observing me as he waited for the adjacent sink to fill with water. I felt acutely embarrassed, doing my very personal washing with him standing there watching over me. He gave me a dazzling grin as I blushed to the roots of my hair.

When the washing had been wrung out to the best of my ability and hung on the lines, we rode off to have a better look at Carnac Plage and the surfers.

The competition must have been happening somewhere else. There were no surfers to be seen, in fact hardly a car or person in sight. Perhaps we should have turned west, not east, when we had reached the shore. The beach didn't look at all inviting and the sea was as grey as the leaden sky. We rode along feeling miserable. When were we going to get a bit more sparkle into this holiday, or at least some sunshine?

Almost a mile up the road we came across a row of pedal boats moored neatly to a jetty. Pete and Malc looked longingly down at them. Pity the place wasn't open for business; everywhere was as dead as a dodo. We stood idly on the jetty, feeling disappointed. Then a voice from behind startled us. We turned to see that there *was* a man in the boat hut after all. He'd probably closed the door to keep the draught out. He put down his newspaper and came over to us.

Hiring a boat wasn't cheap, but the boys deserved a treat. I wanted to make it up to Malc for leaving him last night, and Pete could certainly do with cheering up, having coped with his wretched toe for the whole holiday. There hadn't been many highlights for them.

They climbed into a boat and set off out to sea, their legs working away like hummingbird wings. As they put the boat through its paces, bobbing up and down on the waves, they seemed more like real buddies than rival siblings. Swerving this way and that, they tried to tip the boat up, laughing like loonies. I hadn't seen Pete so happy for ages. With their 'flat-top' haircuts and the big grins on their faces they looked like a pair of Stan Laurels (they used to love watching Laurel and Hardy on TV). Malc had copied Pete's hairstyle a couple of months earlier, much to Pete's great annoyance.

The man in the hut let them have extra time, which was kind. But then he didn't have a queue of people waiting for a turn. We returned in a much lighter mood, though it was hard work cycling into wind, especially as the boys' legs were aching from pedalling the boat so hard.

Malc came with me to the supermarket, leaving Pete to explore the local shops. I then decided to hang around town until 6 pm (English time) in order to ring Jim. I thought it might be a cheaper rate by then. Pete offered to go back and pick some blackberries for tea, since I'd just bought an enormous cooking apple to stew for a pudding. Blackberries would go nicely with it. There were loads of juicy ones hanging high up on the hedgerow near our tent. I supposed Pete could reach them.

At last I succeeded in getting through to Jim. He said he was fine and also that Granddad had improved. Great news! Now we must hurry back for supper. Malc and I couldn't wait; we were famished. Tonight it was going to be beef casserole and potatoes, followed by apple and blackberries, sweetened with the blackberry syrup I'd just bought in the supermarket. I wasted no time in peeling the potatoes. Cut into small pieces, they cooked fairly quickly on our little stove. I carefully balanced the saucepan of beef casserole on top, to heat at the same time. Within half an hour we were eating our first course, but we had to wait a while longer for pudding. I still had the apple to peel.

One of our neighbouring campers told us he'd been to the Quiberon peninsula that day, and recommended it to us. After dinner we got out the map to see exactly where it was, hoping the weather would buck up.

The washing was still wet in spite of the strong wind which had been blowing all day. Should I leave it out all night or bring it in? I took the lazy option and left it. I boiled water for the ritual bedtime toe soaking then made two beakers of Nesquik with hot milk for Pete and myself (Malc didn't want one). I thought it might be more sleep-inducing than wine. But alas, the horse in the next field kept me awake half the night with its constant neighing.

CHAPTER ELEVEN

Return of the sun

Quiberon and the road to Concarneau

Although the strong wind had dropped, the next morning was another disappointingly dull one; cold and misty, not at all the sort of day to spend by the sea. But as we ate our breakfast under the flysheet, which Pete had propped open with a long stick, we realised that the misty clouds were slowly getting thinner. Soon we could see the pale disc of the sun.

An hour later we were sitting outside the tents in warm sunshine watching the clouds slowly evaporating into the blue sky. We savoured it for a while, feeling the sun's rays getting hotter and hotter on our skin. Wow! This was what we'd come on holiday for. The tide was turning. We'd better not sit here a moment longer - the Quiberon peninsula was calling us.

I jumped on my bike and dashed to the supermarket. We'd need to take food with us. I returned with only a baguette, a large cucumber at a bargain price and a large packet of biscuits. Not very much for a day out, but I was being frugal after spending our food money on the pedal boat yesterday. I strapped my swimming things and the bread to the top of my pannier rack, snapped the cucumber in half and stuffed it into my handlebar bag together with the biscuits, then we raced off in happy anticipation to find the coastal road.

Riding westwards out of Carnac Plage we made a big loop around the bay. The sea looked very shallow and silted up at this northerly end. From here the road went due south down the peninsula. We stopped to look at an historic, wooden ship on the eastern side of the spit. It was propped up with thick wooden supports and served as a museum. But we didn't go inside

A railway line ran alongside the road for a while. I wasn't sure whether it was redundant or not but felt quite worried, as several children were playing on it.

At one point the peninsula was barely wider than the road. Perhaps Quiberon had been a separate island once. I wondered if the tide ever came in to cut the peninsula off from the mainland, but I couldn't see any tidemarks or traces.

The main road kept its straight, flat course southwards and as the land mass widened out, it didn't seem that we were on a peninsula at all. As we rode through the small town of Saint Pierre, tantalizing smells of fish and chips wafted by. Here we turned westwards towards the village of Kergroix. The eastern side had seemed rather boring. Now we were on a narrow, undulating road, leading down to the west coast.

Gee whiz! A magnificent coastline stretched out in front of us. As we stood on top of the rocky cliffs, gazing out over the Bay of Biscay, the waves came pounding in with a tremendous force. No wonder they called it Le Côte Sauvage (the wild coast). To both the north and south we could see small sandy bays. The sun was hot, the sea sparkled and we felt extremely happy.

We continued riding southwards down the coast, where the cliffs became gradually lower. Now they were covered with lovely short grass, no taller than moss, and full of pretty little flowers. This was an ideal place for a picnic. We lounged on the soft, green sward, seeing who could count the most different species of flowers as we ate our bread and cucumber. It was so scorching hot that this seemed enough food to satisfy us right now. We allowed ourselves a couple of biscuits each then kept the rest for later. We also had to be frugal with our water. There was nowhere to get a drink.

The coastline was flattening out so we turned back, to head in the opposite direction. It looked wilder to the north. There were no toilets to be seen and with only barren cliff tops, just nothing to hide behind. I was getting desperate.

The first bay we came to had a treacherously steep path. We carried on. When we reached the third bay there were people swimming in the sea. The track to the beach was far too steep and narrow to wheel the bikes down, so we locked them up at the top. I hastily changed into my swimming things (under my towel – I was such a prude). Nobody was in sight and the boys were looking over the cliff. They were already in their swimming shorts. They'd been cycling in them all day.

It wasn't until we reached the beach that we saw a sign saying that swimming was prohibited. We hesitated briefly

Posing with Malc on the edge of the cliffs at Le Côte Sauvage

Pete, too near the whirlpool and struggling to keep upright
in the sea at Le Côte Sauvage

then thought, "If they can do it, so can we." Anyway, I couldn't wait a moment longer.

What fearsome waves! Malc and I were really intimidated but Pete waded straight in, bold as brass. We followed, full of trepidation. It was a battle to push through the water and almost impossible to stand up. We could easily have been dashed onto the shore.

Pete was in his element from the word 'go' and once we'd got used to it, Malc and I relaxed and began to enjoy ourselves. If the other people hadn't been in the water already, we would never have dared to swim here. Actually, we didn't do much swimming. It was more fun in the surf. I saw a swirling whirlpool nearby. Crikey! We'd have to keep clear of that.

Later, after going on shore a few times to take photos, I became a bit complacent. A rogue wave caught me unawares, knocking me sideways. I stumbled clumsily, treading heavily on Pete's toe as the force of water threw me over on top of him. He groaned in pain as we went down and were swept several feet up the beach. Spluttering and coughing we managed to stand up before the next wave got us. I helped Pete out of the water. He was limping like a wounded soldier, which made me feel awful. The three of us sat on the beach, hoping his toe would soon stop throbbing. We still had to cycle back to Carnac Plage.

As we sat waiting, a flurry of wind caught the sand and flung it straight up into Malc's face. He cried out, clawing at his eyes and rubbing in the sand even more. I slapped his hands and shouted for him to stop. He'd only make matters worse. Then I carefully washed out his eyes with water from my bottle. Afterwards, they were still sore and gritty and made him feel miserable.

Now I had two invalids to cope with. However, the brief distraction had taken Pete's mind off his toe for a moment and he was able to hobble back up the cliff path.

The return journey was a sober affair, but we had to get back before 7.30pm, when the shops would be closing. In St. Pierre we passed the lovely smell of fish and chips again. It made us feel really hungry. The boys shared the rest of their water with me and we speeded up a little, now that we were back on the long straight peninsula road.

Back in Carnac Plage, Malc made straight for the campsite to see to his sore eyes. I promised to wash them out again, as soon as I returned from the supermarket. Pete was recovered enough to come shopping with me. I was very relieved not to have done lasting damage to his toe.

As we rode back into the campsite the proprietress beckoned us over to the office. I'd completely forgotten that I owed her for another night. I dutifully paid up.

Outside the tent I had another go at flushing Malc's eyes. They still looked just as red and sore afterwards but he said they felt slightly better. I couldn't think what else I could do for him right now, so I set about peeling the remainder of the potatoes. I fried them, thinly sliced, with a few strips of streaky bacon and some eggs. There was no second course tonight.

The moon was big and bright. Hoping to get an artistic photo of it, I took the camera outside. But it felt very creepy, standing near the big shadowy hedges. Images of that intruder outside our tent kept flashing through my mind, even though it had turned out to be Malc. I changed my mind and hurried back inside, shivering.

* * * * *

They had only sterilised milk at the shop early that morning, so we had to eat our Weetabix with milk that none of us liked. I'd bought bread, biscuits and eggs for our evening meal. We didn't want to be caught out on a Sunday night with no shops open. Luckily, we had a plastic egg-carrying case with us.

We were heading for Rosporden today, which was back the way we'd come, plus twenty-six miles extra. Our intended destination, which would take us two days to reach, was Pentrez Plage, with the long sandy beach we'd enjoyed so much the previous year. The route we were taking would miss out the busy city of Quimper. We could hardly wait to be on that beach again.

The plan was to have an early start. We'd been to the shops as soon as they'd opened. But by the time we'd said cheerio to the people we'd become acquainted with and had packed up everything, it was 11 am. We were passing the rows of menhirs when it began to rain, just spitting and spotting at first. We didn't stop, as we needed to make good progress after our late start. However, by the time we'd reached the long, flat bridge of the estuary, we'd donned our anoraks, as the rain had become persistent. As we progressed across this vast expanse of water the wind picked up. "Here we go again," I thought.

I was at the front today, letting my two invalids have a break, but already I felt tired. Malc's eyes were still quite sore. He was tucked in behind me for shelter. Pete seemed fairly quiet and detached. I think we were all feeling peed-off with the weather and perhaps a bit sunstroked from yesterday.

My chain came off while I was changing gear and Malc put it back on for me. Then we sat in a nearby bus shelter for a while and ate biscuits. We had to force ourselves out into the rain again. Another five miles and we'd be at Hennebont.

We negotiated a sharp bend under a railway bridge, to be confronted by traffic lights in front of some roadworks. The lights changed to red as we came round the bend, making us brake sharply and skid to a halt. Using this idle time, we stood in a little huddle, checking the map which was under the plastic of Pete's bar-bag, casually eating sweets in a mindless fashion.

Suddenly a car came screeching round the corner and crunched into the car alongside us. We were jolted back to reality. As the occupants of both cars got out to remonstrate with each other, the lights changed to green. We rode off and left them to it. There was nothing we could do. However, this incident made us a bit more wary. It might have been us who'd been hit.

We continued through Pont Scorff to Quimperlé, hardly believing this was the same route we'd sped along so happily only three days earlier. It was hard work into the wind, but at long last the rain was beginning to ease.

Our route took us right past the municipal campsite where we'd stayed the previous Wednesday night. Malc and I went in to refill our water bottles from a tap. We ate the last of our biscuits and had another look at the map. Then I realised that if we kept due west, on the D783, we could actually cycle to Concarneau instead of turning off for Rosporden. It would be about the same distance. I asked the boys what they thought. They ummed and aahed awhile, then agreed. So at last I would get to see Concarneau.

I took them to a café and treated them to a coffee each, which unfortunately tasted horrible. When we came out, the sun was shining and the wind had eased. Things were looking up.

We had to push our bikes up a steep hill. No sooner had we reached the top than we heard the dreaded creak and crack; Pete's pannier rack had broken again. It was the other side that had gone this time. Another delay! But Pete set about mending it in the very same way he'd used the first time; the flat spanner, insulation tape and a screwdriver. It didn't seem quite so catastrophic this time.

Twenty minutes later we were on the road again. When we passed a large garage in the middle of nowhere we suddenly felt hungry. No wonder, we'd existed on nothing but sweets and biscuits all day. It was now five o'clock. The garage prices were extortionate, but even so we bought a large packet of crisps and a bottle of juice. These we devoured standing on the forecourt before continuing towards Concarneau.

Soon we'd reached Pont-Aven, a small town which had been favoured by impressionist painters, including Gauguin, a century before (I'd read that in my book). In the evening sunshine it looked charming. It was quite easy to see why artists would be attracted to it – a town of mellow-stoned houses nestling against a wooded hillside, with a river running through the centre, traversed by a quaint stone bridge. I was impressed by how the new buildings had been blended in with the old ones, using the same sort of materials but with a modern slant.

The fast-flowing little river ran beneath the bridge we were on and the boys climbed down to see if there were any fish in the water. Once this stream had powered many mills, but now the town was solely a tourist attraction.

Time was getting on. We still had several miles to cycle to reach my Concarneau and we'd be arriving in the dark at this rate. As we continued westwards the low sun was absolutely blinding. After the earlier incident in Hennebont, I was more conscious of the risks to our safety. "Please God, let the car drivers see us from behind," I whispered, not sure if I was truly a believer. But only two more cars passed us on the rest of the journey, and they obviously saw us.

The sun was setting as we rode into Concarneau. We passed a harbour surrounded by factories, which were probably to do with the fish-canning industry. I felt SO disappointed to be entering the town by the tradesman's entrance. And because it was getting late, there was no way we could go looking round the old town now. I'd have to wait until morning. Therefore, we continued riding round the back of town on the main road to find the designated campsite on the other side.

It looked more like a forest than a campsite as we cycled in through an avenue of tall sweet chestnut trees. But the reception office was closed for the night, and we couldn't book a plot if there was nobody to pay.

When the avenue split into two tracks we took the lower one to the left. There were small clearings at regular intervals, most of them empty. We finally chose a plot about a quarter of a mile further down. The boys got straight on with their tasks before it got too dark, while I set up the cooker. After a Cuppa Soup each, we had omelettes with bread.

That night, I was back in Malc's tent. He seemed quite happy about that, in fact I felt he preferred it to being on his own. I still had a little wine left over from our first night in Carnac Plage and gave Pete half a beaker of it. He retired to bed without soaking his toe. He couldn't be bothered to wait for the kettle to boil. We were all worn out.

In Malc's tent I shared my beakerful of wine with him while we made up silly jokes and laughed a lot. His eyes were feeling better. It was a good end to a long day.

* * * * *

Malc and I were jolted awake by car doors banging very close by. Looking at my luminous travel clock, I read 6.30, so I'd had a good night's sleep.

Minutes later we heard a siren whirring and whining, building up to a great crescendo until the air was filled with its loud wailing. "Is there a war on?" rasped Malc, in alarm and confusion. I was equally confused but didn't know what to think. Then as the siren sound fell lower and lower until it was almost a growl, a new noise took over; myriads of scooters, all buzzing into Concarneau like a swarm of angry bees. "I reckon they must be calling out the lifeboat, Malc" I concluded.

Down in the town the scooter activity faded into silence. We wondered who was in peril and hoped they'd be rescued. But our worrying wouldn't help them, so we tried to relax and snuggled into our sleeping bags.

Then a sudden, shrill shriek right above our heads made our eyes pop and our hair stand on end. We were frightened to death. It was as if we were in a jungle, what with big drops of rainwater plop plopping from the trees that hung over us and now this frightful, unrecognisable noise.

A clap of heavy wings startled us all over again, and then from further away came the same piercing call. It was like a "pee-whit" sound but the "whit" bit was a long, high-pitched and ear-splitting "Wheeeee".

Owls began to hoot all over the place. It felt so spooky. We were wide-awake now and on the verge of panicking. There were probably witches on broomsticks flying through the trees!

We did our best to calm down, trying to ignore the noises all around us, tossing and turning to get comfy. The wet edges of our sleeping bags were creeping inwards so that there was less and less dry space to lie on, but I think Malc did go back to sleep, eventually.

I went on turning over and over, getting colder and colder. Why wasn't it light yet? I looked at my clock again – 4.20 am.

Then it dawned on me. Last time I must have had my clock upside down. So I'd been awake for hours. When morning eventually arrived we were both freezing.

From where our tents were pitched we couldn't see much sky through the tree cover. One minute there was a window of beautiful blue sky, with the sun's rays filtering through the leaves then, a minute later it was grey again and the rain was spitting down. We wouldn't know the overall weather prospects until we were out in the open.

On my early visit to the ladies' washroom, I was taken aback when a man walked briskly in to fit a pipe onto a tap. Luckily I was fully clothed. Supposing he must be the proprietor, I greeted him with a swift "Bonjour", then ducked my head down quickly to splash water on my face. I didn't want him to remember what I looked like because I was feeling guilty that we hadn't booked in yet. He kept coming in and out, so I was forced to dash into a loo in my various states of undress each time he entered. I felt so annoyed that I decided to avoid paying him for our stay. It had been such a dire experience anyway.

Back at the tent I made each of us a cup of black coffee. That's all we had left. We'd have to find a supermarket before we could eat.

We became aware of two young men standing in the avenue, staring at us. I thought they might be checking us out, but Pete said they were camping in the plot below us. Perhaps they were just curious as to how we'd pack everything onto our bikes.

Minutes later, when they'd disappeared from sight, we heard blood-curdling screams coming from the direction of their tent. We carried on packing in a pretend nonchalant way, hoping that it was just a bit of fun going on in there, and not murder. Happily, two couples emerged before we left at 11 o'clock.

We couldn't decide whether to walk out casually pushing our bikes or tear out, riding them. We opted for walking and made our way back through the trees, along the same tracks that we'd come in on. But when we reached the junction signposted Reception, we couldn't hold back any longer. Jumping on the bikes we pedalled like fury out of the campsite and down the hill, where the boys turned right, *away* from Concarneau. Now all my hopes of exploring Concarneau were well and truly dashed. The boys wouldn't want to backtrack, just for me to look at a *town* and I certainly didn't want to drag them back purely on a whim. One day, perhaps, I'd get another chance, although I realised that Concarneau didn't hold such a rosy picture in my mind as it had before.

At the first bend we were confronted by a steep incline. I had to get off and push, thus slowing our quick getaway.

We pedalled along a fairly scenic coastal road towards Fouesnant but after a few miles the pleasure was marred by foul smells of sewage. As we continued through the Forêt de Fouesnant another daunting hill loomed. Just looking at it made me feel tired. Luckily though, before we'd even changed down gear to tackle it, we saw a signpost pointing left, for Quimper. That's where we were heading (the city we'd planned to avoid).

We still had a steep winding climb. But it was doable, which was fortunate because several large lorries passed us, leaving little room for a walking cyclist with a wide load (had I been one!)

The good news was that all the clouds were missing us, so we hadn't needed to put our anoraks on. The downside was that we hadn't seen a single shop. In fact I don't think we'd even passed any houses since leaving the campsite.

At a crossroads on the brow of a bare hill we saw a 'left' sign for a supermarket. Another left sign a mile up the road led us even further off our intended route and still there was no sign of civilization. We eventually arrived at a row of modern little shops next to a large car park. Nearby was a cluster of new houses. We could have been anywhere in England, I thought. There was a supermarket, a hairdresser's, an electrical shop, a clothes shop and a newsagent's, catering for all the basic needs of this community. I wouldn't have wanted to live here, in this isolated, treeless, featureless place, completely lacking in character and heritage.

Still, no time for my hoity-toity aesthetics. It was mid-day and we were desperately hungry, not having eaten since yesterday evening. Perhaps it was because of this and because of last night's free camping, that I went overboard with my purchases. I bought so much that we didn't know what to do with it all.

We stood in the car park stuffing ourselves until we felt almost sick. The huge baguette we ripped apart and filled with crisps and cheese slices, followed by two Danish pastries apiece. We drank some fruit juice and continued with bananas, nectarines and apples, then opened the chocolate biscuits. We couldn't manage the raisins or peanuts, which were in containers almost as big as shoes. These I forced into my handlebar bag, stretching the stitches to breaking point. Other leftovers, including bars of chocolate and a small jar of coffee, were strapped here, there and anywhere as best we could.

None of us felt like cycling back up to the main road, although once we were on it we sailed along. The wind was cool, but when the sun came out it felt quite hot. We were constantly stopping to take clothes off or to put them back on again. Malc was the worst. He was either stripped to the waist with shorts on, or all coddled up in anorak and tracksuit bottoms. Pete and I had to keep waiting for him while he laboriously took off his shoes, untying and retying the shoelaces every single time.

There were frequent signs advertising the Quimper Hypermarché we'd visited last year. We'd toyed with the idea of going there again, but it wasn't on our route. We weren't prepared to do any detours now, especially as we were full to bursting and had spent so much money.

The traffic was very heavy on the outskirts of the city, where we had to negotiate a massive roundabout. We felt extremely vulnerable on two wheels in the fast traffic, not quite sure where to position ourselves in the lanes. Our fears were realised when a speeding van cut straight across my path to take a right hand turn, just missing my front wheel. I gasped with fright and escaped shakily into the next turning, although it wasn't our intended one. Thankfully the boys were still behind me, but I felt I was risking our lives because of my selfish whims.

The little road we found ourselves on led through the suburbs of Quimper. We wandered about not really knowing which way to go but feeling safer now we were off the main route. Quimper was in a hollow. Pete didn't want us to go all the way down there, only to have to climb out again. But we'd have to, as we needed to head off on the opposite side to get to Pentrez Plage.

A big shower caught us unawares as we debated where to go. There was nowhere to shelter and we couldn't get our anoraks on quickly enough. I pressed myself against a privet hedge. On the other side of it a woman looked up through her kitchen window and grinned at me. I don't know what she had to smile about – all her washing was out on the line getting soaked.

When this burst of rain was over we splashed down the hill to the city and the sun reappeared and warmed us once again. We pushed the bikes along the riverside towards the cathedral, which I was determined to see now that we'd come here again. We were also looking out for a post office. I had cards to send that I'd bought in Carnac but still hadn't managed to buy stamps for, let alone find a post box. (Just as well, really. I hadn't even written them yet!)

By the time we reached the cathedral it was raining again. We quickly slipped through an archway for shelter and sat on a narrow ledge in semi-darkness. Here I wrote my postcards while we quietly nibbled the chocolate. Groups of sightseers were being led through, not even noticing us. But when I suddenly looked up from my writing, a man almost jumped out of his skin. He probably thought he'd just seen the ghosts of three hooded monks. Everyone had a good laugh over it.

When the rain stopped, Pete saw a *tabac* in the distance and I trotted off, crossing several sets of traffic lights, to buy some stamps. There was still no sign of a post box though.

I didn't look inside the cathedral after all. I'd just read that the towers were added in the mid 19th Century and that spoilt it for me. In hindsight I was stupid, because when I read the whole paragraph later, I found that the cathedral was rated as one of the finest in Brittany. Viewed from a distance, it did indeed look magnificent.

We set off again up a steep climb, just as Pete had said it would be, and we could now remember it from the previous year. What seemed like a mile out and still climbing in a built-up street, we stopped at a small shop to buy a drink. The cheapest was a huge bottle of Coca Cola. We shared it into our three bottles and drank the rest. When I took the bottle back to ask the lady if she would kindly dispose of it, she surprised me by handing over 25c in return. I asked if she knew of any postboxes nearby but she didn't. We kept a constant look out all the same.

Now we were cycling towards Locronan, with plenty of hills to make us sweat. No sooner had we taken our anoraks off than it rained again.

However, the sun was gorgeous as we rode into the town. To us Locronan was just a small place on the map, but masses of people were milling about everywhere. There were lots of craft-like shops on either side of the road. Then we turned a corner and found ourselves in a beautiful square. Wow! This was like stepping back in history. (It had hardly changed since the Renaissance, I read.) There were lovely old buildings surrounding the cobbled square, from which led five small roads. The main one snaked across the middle, delineated by cobbles of a slightly different hue. I thought the cars looked out of place, although they were crawling through.

Pete didn't really want to stop. According to him, we'd been stopping all day. But I didn't mind. I hadn't got much vim in me today. We leaned our bikes against the side of the church and sat on a low wall to take in the scene.

A constant stream of people was emerging from a quaint café on the other side of the square. They were holding ice creams in dainty little cones, which looked very appetising. I offered to get us one each, but Pete thought I'd be wasting my money. I went over all the same and chose three of various flavours as a treat. They *were* tiny. What a rip off! They were gone in three bites. I should have listened to my son.

The films in both our cameras had run out at Carnac. Unable to stop myself from spending, I decided to have just one more splurge and buy a film. Then we could take photos of this lovely town. Malc and I went all round the shops and finally found films for sale at the back of a bar. It cost us almost F30. Diabolical! I must have spent all the money we'd saved the previous night twice over. Anyway, while we'd been gone, Pete had found a post box for me.

The next town, Plonevez-Porzay, didn't look at all impressive after Locronan, except that the church had large ornate handles sticking out from each corner of its tower.

To avoid cycling in a big right-angle to get to our destination, we tried to negotiate small back roads which were hard to follow on the map. We were searching for a left turn to St. Sébastien. However, as we couldn't see any signs we took pot luck at the next turning. Now we needed to get the map out at every single junction. It might have been quicker if we'd stuck to the main road.

From a high point, I was the first to see the sea. It didn't look very inviting, just a grey blob. But at least we were heading the right way.

The next turning led us down a bumpy lane which terminated at a farm. On the long toil back, we passed a woman out walking a dog and asked her for directions. She gave us such a complicated route; back to the main road then on to somewhere called Plomodiern. (Recognising the name, I realised that this was the route we were trying to avoid). So we plodded on the way we'd been going. At least we knew it was in the right direction.

There was a horrible brownish-black cloud heading our way, although right now we were in warm sunshine and could see a patch of sea again. This time it was sparkling blue. I was glad Malc hadn't seen it first time round.

A little further on we came to a junction where we turned left, almost sure it would be the right way. It was narrow and hilly. The ominous cloud was getting nearer. We were in an elevated and exposed position with nowhere to shelter. We'd probably get soaked before long.

At the next steep hill I got off to walk. Malc, behind me, followed suit, while Pete toiled on ahead. He still had enough energy. But when I rounded the bend and saw that he hadn't made much progress, I thought I'd try to catch him up and surprise him. The hill was less steep now.

With immense effort I was closing the gap between Pete and myself when suddenly, a car came flying over the brow of the hill and swerved zigzaggedly past. Immediately behind flashed another car. It just missed us. There was a thud and a shattering of glass. Pete and I swung round in horror, thinking that Malc had been hit. But, thank goodness, he was still standing by the roadside, only a few feet from the crash scene. He did look rather shaken.

A longhaired youth got out of the second car, which was now crumpled at the front with its lights smashed in. However, both drivers seemed to be unscathed. They inspected the damage. Very self-consciously, we stood by, feeling implicated even though we'd done nothing wrong. The two drivers ignored us completely and, to our astonishment, got back into their cars and *reversed* past us up the hill, where they continued their discussion. As we rode sheepishly past, they didn't so much as look at us. Phew!

I shared my few remaining sweets with the boys. Malc seemed to be recovering quite quickly from his close shave, although he was a bit quiet.

While we'd been distracted, the big black cloud had miraculously missed us. Now the sea and the sky were both beautifully blue as far as the eye could see.

We sped down a very steep hill towards the Bay of Douarnenez, arriving at the southerly end of Pentrez Plage. It was like old times – sunny and breezy. Another couple of miles along the beach-side road brought us to our old campsite, Menez Bichen. We were smiling now. The prospects were looking good.

In the office I booked in for two nights, although I hoped we'd afford to stop for three. Pete and Malc wanted to camp in exactly the same spot as last year. I grumbled that the noise of the sea was likely to keep me awake. So the boys trudged with me up to the next plot then the next, trying to choose a better place. We went on past the toilet block, right round and down the other side. It seemed too lonely up at the top; no caravans or tents at all. So I relented and said I'd go near to the bottom end after all. We settled for one plot higher than last year but put the tents in exactly the same position, in front of the hedge in the evening sunshine.

While we were unpacking everything I realised that Malc and I had damp sleeping bags. How lucky to have this warm sunshine to dry them in. Once the tents were erected we lay the sleeping bags over the top.

Opposite us, in a shady corner, we could see a woman and two children watching us from under the awning of their caravan. They probably wondered why we'd chosen to camp so near to them, with all our untidiness, when we had the whole site to choose from.

Discovering my wet sleeping bag as Malc and I unpack at Pentrez Plage

I left the boys to tidy up while I went to catch the shop before 7.30 pm. There was plenty of time. I had a nostalgic stroll through the top of the site, past the farm and through the gate to the local shop.

It seemed as if I was buying rather a lot, but I was getting food to last for more than one day. I thought if I did more cooking, I could fill us up more cheaply. So I picked up a box of rice, a bulb of garlic and a small tin of curry paste. On the Carnac site we had often passed a caravan from which the most tantalisingly spicy smells drifted. Just because we couldn't afford to eat out and had only a little camping stove, it didn't mean that we couldn't add a little spice to our food.

To go with my rice I chose bacon pieces, courgettes and tomatoes, then put the usual necessities into my basket. The bread had sold out so I got *toastinettes* instead, which were like rusks and we loved them. I even bought margarine for Pete and myself and it didn't matter how strapped for cash we were, I wasn't going to forgo my wine. I bought the very cheapest at 50p and some lemonade to sweeten it up a bit.

That evening I made a lovely bacon fried rice to which we added curry paste. Malc had the tiniest amount, which made him gasp and drink loads of water. But Pete and I had a good teaspoonful each and thoroughly enjoyed it.

Unfortunately, I put the hot frying pan down on the ground sheet and burned a hole in it. The plastic stuck to the bottom of the pan like rock.

Afterwards, we strolled over to the beach. We were surprised to see the water right up to the wall. Last year it hadn't come nearly so high, at least not while we'd been staying there.

Further along the beach was a climbing frame and a roundabout, both fixed into the ground. The higher tides were in the process of wrecking them. Between the waves, Malc jumped onto the roundabout and helped the sea with its destruction.

That night I just couldn't sleep. The noise of the sea drove me to distraction. Around 6 am I groped around for my paracetamol tablets and took a couple with lemonade. I relaxed a little then (probably the placebo effect) and dozed off for a while.

Pentrez Plage revisited

Pete was up and dressed quite early, in anticipation of a good day, I think. He went to the shop for some milk but was told it wouldn't arrive until 10.30 am. Someone suggested he might try the farmhouse instead. So he came back and washed out our water bottles and took them up to the farm to be filled with milk.

Malc woke up eventually to say he'd had an awful night because he was lying on a bump. I assured him we'd do something about it later on.

We ate the last of our Weetabix. The sugar had already run out and we wouldn't be replacing it.

Outside, the sky was dull, the wind was cool and we were bitterly disappointed. We hadn't imagined there'd be anything but sunshine at Pentrez Plage. In fact when we'd left England we'd been expecting wall-to-wall sunshine to make up for all the lousy weather back home. That's why people went abroad. But here we were, on the twelfth day of our holiday, and we'd had only one whole day that was hot, plus the odd hour here and there. The bad weather seemed to have followed us from England.

The boys moped about in their tents, Pete doing crossword puzzles and Malc drawing cartoons, while I got on with a load of washing (including eight more pairs of white socks, although if Tom had been with us it would have been twelve pairs). My little tablet of Vanish did vanish and I had to finish off with washing-up liquid.

About midday, after I'd hung out the washing, we went down to the beach to see if the water was warm enough to paddle in. The tide was right out this time. Malc was really disappointed because the beach was so wet. He couldn't even make a sand sculpture. We walked towards the sea but our shoes were getting soaked. It wasn't even warm enough to go barefoot, let alone paddle in the sea.

Feeling bored, we ambled back to the tents, where Pete resumed his crosswords as if he'd never left them. Malc, ever ready to create a bit of fun, asked me if I'd have a game of table tennis with him. Baffled as to what we'd play with, I followed him down to the games room, where he produced one of those very small, very bouncy balls. He'd bought it in Roscoff.

There were three table-tennis tables in the games room. This room opened into a TV room at the other end.

Using our hands as bats, we had an absolutely hilarious game of table tennis. It was virtually impossible to hit the ball, let alone keep a score, and the ball went any which way but the way you thought it would. Not only that, the games room was dimly lit and both the floor and the ball were speckled red. When we looked down for the ball it would bounce up and hit us on the nose.

We were falling about with laughter; in fact Malc was getting more fun from mimicking me. Eventually, when we'd tired ourselves completely, we went back up to the tents. I was sorry that Pete had missed out on the fun.

If Malc were to get a good night's sleep, we'd need to sort the tent out. We hadn't lined them up very well yesterday, anyway. So we moved the bell end over a few inches, which straightened them out a bit. I hoped it would make a difference.

I rode up to the shop at the top and broke yesterday's resolution that I'd do more cooking. Now that I'd worn myself out I couldn't even be bothered to set up the stove. Earlier, I'd bought a lovely crusty baguette in the camp shop and now I quite fancied salad in it. So I bought the mangy-looking cucumber I'd walked past the day before, plus a couple of soft tomatoes and a rather tired-looking lettuce. The shop was having a very slow turnover now that the season was coming to an end. I pitied anyone who relied on it during the winter months. Finally I bought a pack containing three slices of ham, plus two litres of milk. We'd taken to having lots of milky drinks lately. It filled us up a bit, although I was becoming mightily sick of both milky coffee and Nesquik, and drank them more as a medicine than a pleasure. I wondered if the boys felt the same.

I almost forgot to buy more plasters for Pete's toe. The choice was limited; assorted ones with hardly any in the packet, or a big roll of plaster with no padding. I chose the big roll, which was more expensive, but we'd have loads left to take home. Pete would just have to use more cotton wool for padding.

We had an early tea. It was nice and easy to prepare with no washing-up afterwards, and it tasted good. As we sat eating it, the young boy and girl from our neighbouring caravan walked past, staring at us. They continued to the edge of the field, turned round, then came back for another look. Not content with that, they called for their friends, two boys from another caravan, and all four walked past to gawp at us. You'd think we were aliens.

After tea, we went down to the beach again. The tide was still quite a way out, but the water on the sand had dried out a bit. We could walk to the edge of the waves now, without getting our shoes wet through.

A rumbling noise above our heads made us look upwards. We were amazed to see a small yellow aeroplane with orange wingtips and tailplane coming through the clouds. It nosed slowly down towards the beach. Whatever was it doing, landing here? Was it involved in something illegal, like smuggling? We felt quite excited, being the only witnesses to this covert mission. As far as the eye could see there was no one else on the beach.

Then, when only a few feet from the ground, its engines revved up and it rose, circled over the road and was gone, heading off in the direction of Brest. Oh well! That was nearly a bit of excitement for us.

Disappointed, we went back to the campsite. The beach seemed quite boring when the sun wasn't shining. It was beautifully flat for playing games on and for windsailing, even for landing planes on. However, apart from the caves at the far southerly end, there wasn't anything of interest; no shells, no seaweed, nothing. I really couldn't understand why, because Pentrez Plage was at the end of the Baie de Douarnenez. I'd have thought that many things would be washed up onto the shore. At least there were no sharp pebbles to stand on if you were swimming. If only!

Back at the tents we messed about, killing time until the tide came in again. Pete seemed to hog the radio and chose all the programmes that we listened to. French radio was always playing lots of English pop tunes, several months after they'd left our charts. Terence Trent d'Arby came on for the umpteenth time, singing *Sign Your Name Across My Heart*. Pete flicked the station over. Surely he knew it was one of my favourites? I felt annoyed. But the next station he picked up was an English one where a Cotswold pub was being discussed. There was controversy surrounding its conversion into flats. It made a change and brought us nearer to home for a while, which was quite comforting as we were feeling rather down in the dumps. While we listened I made us an omelette sandwich each, with garlic in it. Pete and I spread curry paste on ours.

When we next went over to the beach the tide was already lashing up the slipway. Our neighbour was there with her two children. They stood on the slipway, daring the waves to catch them. Pete and Malc, being older, had to go a step further than that to impress them. They climbed onto the wet boulders that made up the sloping sea defence, and tried to get their feet onto the sand in between each wave. I thought they were stupid with the sea being so rough and the boulders being so slippery, but they needed a bit of a challenge. I just hoped they wouldn't break their ankles. The neighbour and I stood at the top, shivering in our anoraks. We were only nodding acquaintances and didn't speak to each other.

Amazingly, further up the bay, a woman was swimming in the sea. How brave of her. How could she bear the cold water and the chilly wind? I wished I'd had her fortitude.

The boys were soon looking for fresh amusement, so we walked along the top of the sea wall to the northerly end, where the waves were crashing into the corner. They stood on the top pretending to lose their balance. The devils! They knew it would make me nervous. I pretended not to care, but inside I was all strung up. I walked away looking for a photo opportunity instead, as I was carrying the camera.

The sun appeared above the horizon, gilding the surface of the sea. It looked beautiful with the dark clouds just above. Perhaps I could take a photo of the boys with the cliffs curving round to the north and the sun setting behind them. I managed to persuade them to pose for me, then walked out into the road, looking through the viewfinder to get the ideal shot.

A Frenchman came along and watched me for a while as I walked forwards and backwards and sideways. Then he shouted "Non, non" and beckoned me over. In the end I went to where he was standing and took a photo from there. By then the boys had stopped posing and were mucking about, making faces. The Frenchman smiled and said it would be "plus naturel." Yes, maybe, but I didn't get my cliffs or my sunset in it. He walked away, looking contented.

Before we settled down in the tent, I placed the bottle of paracetamol tablets next to my feet, in case I wanted some in the night. Malc called me a 'druggie.' However I didn't hear the sea at all that night because it was really windy with occasional squally rain.

Malc told me that he was still lying on a bump. Since we'd moved the tent over, my side of the tent was feeling quite lumpy as well.

* * * * *

If I put my face to the very edge of the tent, I could see out underneath the flysheet. The sky looked miserable. I didn't want to get up. I couldn't stand the thought of yet another dull day. I'd had enough of them. I'd rather stay in bed.

Then, as I lay there, the inside of the tent appeared to be getting brighter. I crawled laboriously from my sleeping bag to look outside. Still cloudy. I snuggled back in. But my curiosity had me looking out several more times. Eventually I spied a small patch of blue sky. 'Enough to make a sailor a pair of trousers,' I thought. By the time the boys woke up there was bright sunshine.

We made plans to spend the morning on the beach. I'd be able to wear my shorts and sun top today. I might even get a tan.

Firstly, I walked down to the camp shop for a baguette. As I was leaving, the lady behind the counter said, "bonne journée." I didn't realise that she was saying, "Have a good day" and thought she'd said "good journey." I sheepishly replied, "Au revoir," knowing that I'd only yet paid for two nights. So by rights, we ought to be on our bikes today. I resolved, right then, that I'd dutifully pay my dues before we left tomorrow morning.

After breakfasting on omelette sandwiches, to which Pete and I added garlic and curry paste, we set off to walk the whole length of the beach, just as we had done on a similar day last year. The tide was right out and there was a good breeze blowing. It wasn't quite as warm as it looked though.

At the other end of the bay were the caves – not cavernous limestone ones but small caves of jagged grey slate, layered diagonally. We paddled about in the rock pools for a while with Pete telling Malc to "mind that crab" all the time. Malc got the jitters and decided to make a sand sculpture instead. It took him ages. While he was doing it, Pete and I passed the time by skimming slates across a rock pool towards each other, to see who could splash the other one the most. Pete was getting really wet, while none of his were wetting me. After a while we realised it was the wind that was doing it. He made me swap sides.

We passed a couple of hours messing about and still Malc hadn't finished. Pete got fed up with waiting and went down

Sunbathing on the only fine morning at Pentrez Plage

Our pitch on the evening before the storm

All coddled up again in my 'puffed-up' anorak

to feel how cold it was in the sea. I helped Malc to clear the spare sand from around his work of art so that we could take a photo. He then asked me to jump on it. I didn't want to, but he insisted. However, after landing on something hard that hurt my foot, I was adamant that if he wanted to destroy it he should do it himself. I think he enjoyed flattening it as much as creating it. But what a shame, after all that hard work!

The sea wasn't very warm. We certainly didn't feel like swimming in it, especially now the sky was clouding over. We wandered slowly back to our end of the beach, wading in the water. Malc wasn't exactly wading; he was hardly wetting the soles of his feet, and all the time he was on a sharp look out for crabs. I told him not to worry because there weren't any on this beach. Ironically, soon after, I felt a definite nip on the foot, but Pete and I didn't mention it to Malc until later. I really don't know why we told him at all. It only made him more wary.

Higher up on the beach, a group of people were digging out worms, like a party of allotment workers – all wellies and forks. They'd turned over a huge rectangle of sand. A man walked down to the shore to warn us of an obstacle ahead; his wife had a long fishing line going out into the sea. We pointedly stepped over it, so that she and her companion could see that we'd missed it. Both women waved to us.

As the day wore on, it became cloudier and windier. We were fed up. Pete made endless alterations and adaptations to the middle flysheet, to provide me with a sheltered canopy for cooking. It felt like wintertime. He draped his sleeping bag on the windward side and secured it with clothes pegs. But while I was boiling milk for hot drinks, it started raining. He whipped the sleeping bag quickly inside. Next, he gave me something to wrap over my legs and a jumper to sit on while I boiled the remainder of our rice. I cut up the three slices of ham I'd bought earlier (the same sort that we'd enjoyed in our baguette yesterday) and mixed it in with the rice. But it tasted horrible like this. Pete and I picked out our ham and ate it first, then mixed curry paste into the rice instead.

I'd bought half a dozen eggs that morning. I was keeping them to eat in Roscoff, either the next day or the one after. That was the very longest our money could last.

Afterwards we went down to the sea for what was now our regular evening on the beach with the tide coming in. Just like the evening before, the clouds cleared on the horizon and revealed the setting sun. The swimmer was in the sea again. She seemed to be in her element. When she finally waded out of the water we saw it was none other than the campsite proprietress. What a woman!

We got into conversation with a man out walking his dog. From his beret down, he looked typically French. But after a while we discovered that he was actually German and his huge dog, Chloe, was also of German extraction. He asked us what route we'd taken on our holiday and couldn't understand where Roscoff was. Then in sudden inspiration he said, "Oh, Rosco." I then assumed that this was how it should be pronounced. However, the next day when I spoke to someone of "Rosco", they hadn't a clue what I was talking about.

Malc and I went back to the tents, leaving Pete in the TV

room. Malc said he found it hard to get to sleep when he was hungry, and he was hungry now, even though it wasn't bedtime. So with slight reluctance I fried him one of our Roscoff eggs. Afterwards, we went down to join Pete. Last year, we didn't even know this games room had existed, probably because we'd spent every day outside in the sun.

With Malc's bouncy ball, the three of us had a rollicking game of table tennis and then went mad, bouncing it from wall to wall and floor to ceiling. We were absolutely creased up with laughing and eventually collapsed on the seats in the TV room to get our breath back.

Surprise surprise, *The Man from Uncle* was on the screen, in French. We sat through it all, trying to understand what was being said. Afterwards came a weather forecast. It looked very ominous over Finistère (the side of Brittany we were in). The weatherman was pulling faces and pushing his hands in the direction of the wind arrows.

We looked at each other dismally and said that we supposed it would be another rotten day tomorrow (or words to that effect!)

I should have slept in Pete's tent that night. But he'd made himself such a wonderful bed. He'd laid his inflated surfboard diagonally across the tent, on top of *all* the clothes that *we* weren't wearing (the cheeky so and so!) He hadn't even asked us if we minded.

But after all Pete's efforts, I decided to sleep in Malc's tent once more. Malc moaned a lot. He said that if it had been him, I'd have made him move his bed over. I couldn't please them all. I just wanted to get some sleep.

Malc and I still had the bumps to sort out. We decided to sleep the other way round with our heads to the opening end. That way, the lumps would be under our legs instead of our ribs. I also swapped sides with him.

Unfortunately our hopes of a decent night's sleep were soon to be dashed.

CHAPTER THIRTEEN

Storm in the night

Pentrez Plage and the return to Roscoff

Soon after we had crawled into our sleeping bags the wind turned increasingly erratic, bringing sudden heavy squalls of rain. The wind and rain increased as the night wore on, torturing our tent. Water began running down the cotton lining, which flapped and billowed alarmingly against my face. I moved my sleeping bag away from the wet edge, holding my body at an uncomfortable angle to avoid rolling onto Malc. I tried to keep this position for two hours or more, thinking yogic thoughts.

From time to time there would be a lull. Each time I thought the storm was abating, but invariably it was followed by a fearful whistling that began far out at sea, getting louder and louder as it roared towards us up the bay. I'd hold my breath, then – SMACK! The wet lining slapped me a stinging blow on the cheek while the tent heaved and sucked as it tried to leave the ground. I was scared stiff, but kept telling Malc (and myself) that it would soon be over. "Gales only last for a few hours" I said.

Around 2 am the tent pole at the bell-end broke apart. It

had had enough. We lay still for a while with half the tent collapsed on top of us like a burst balloon. What the hell were we going to do now? I unzipped the door and shouted across the middle, "We'll have to come into your tent, Pete. Ours has had it." I didn't know if we'd all fit in, considering that Pete had most of our stuff in there already.

Rummaging in the bucking frenzy of the inner sanctum, I found the anoraks. Malc and I struggled to put ours on in a near prone position, hopelessly trying not to touch the top or sides of our soggy tent. Then, using our backs to hold up the roof, we took turns to put our sleeping bags into their dustbin liners, together with anything else we could feel on the floor, such as the pack of cards, phrase books and my paracetamol. We knotted the bags and laid them, knot side down, on the camping mats. At least they wouldn't get any wetter than they already were.

Meanwhile, unknown to us, brave Pete had gone outside to try to secure our tent. As he'd emerged into the raging storm he'd seen a large shape looming towards him through the blackness of the sheeting rain. He'd leapt backwards into the tent, wet and panting. Only then did Malc and I know that he'd even been outside. We peered out and saw a large dog coming towards us. Thinking it might have rabies (there had been an incident in France that year) we cowered behind the meagre protection of our turbulent flysheet, trembling all over.

Now the dog was right outside. It whined. We peeped out again and saw it was a very large collie. It didn't sound at all threatening. We exhaled with relief! Was it Lassie coming to our rescue? More likely it needed to be rescued, for it seemed to want our company.

"Come on, Pete, we can't stay here any longer. We'll have to go up and shelter in the toilet block" I said. After he'd put his sleeping bag into its dustbin liner, we prised ourselves out into the wicked night. The force of rain that suddenly poured down on us was unbelievable. We gasped for breath as we fought our way across the field. The dog followed close behind.

When we turned to make our way up the drive, we were physically blown up to the toilets. The door to the ladies' was thrashing open and shutting continuously so we went round to the men's side to see if that was any better. Once inside, the door slammed shut on us. We stood by the sinks, wet to the skin, shaking. We didn't have a clue what we should do next.

The windows rattled, the door strained on its mountings and the roof sounded as if it would take off at any moment. However, the dog was our distraction. He kept licking our wet hands, wet feet, clothes, everything. We thought he must be thirsty. We filled a sink with water and tried to lift his great hulking front-end up to drink. But he wouldn't. So I emptied the contents of a waste bin down a toilet and filled that with water. He wouldn't drink from that either and kept on licking us.

When we noticed a big sore on his leg we didn't want to touch him any more and kept washing our hands. Although he was a handsome dog with a magnificent ruff, his fur felt horrible to touch. It was thick, like a Husky's and stood up in stark spikes, full of water. Each time he shook himself we were spattered all over with stinky doggy-smelling droplets.

We were soaked already, now we felt unclean as well. But he *was* distracting us from the storm.

Oh to be in a warm dry bed! We felt dreadful, just standing on the cold, draughty concrete floor, waiting for the roof to blow off. Pete and Malc wanted to go over to the new toilet block across on the other side, to see if that was any better. I thought they were raving mad, but I wasn't going to be left here on my own.

Pete went first. The wind wrenched the door from his hand and bashed it against the outside wall. That alone was scary. We slammed it shut behind us and picked our way carefully along the road, doubled over, battling against the elements.

When we reached the new toilet block, we could tell before we'd entered, that it would be even noisier than the old block. The whole wall on one side was constructed of folding wooden doors. They rattled and juddered like a goods train on a bumpy track. Water was surging in underneath them. We didn't hang about.

With great relief we reached the safety of the men's washroom once again, more soaked than ever. The collie stayed close by. Once inside, he shook himself vigorously all over us.

Pete wanted to go and check the tents, but I told him it would be pointless. There was nothing he could do. So he went into the first toilet, which was in the half-light, and sat on the seat. He kept nodding off. I felt jealous. I wanted to sit down, but all the other toilets were in almost complete darkness and Malc and I felt too scared to sit on those, especially with the black voids of the shower cubicles facing them. Anyway they stank. So we just stood there. Eventually the dog stopped licking us and lay on the floor, licking the sore on his leg instead.

The storm seemed to be getting wilder still. We couldn't bear the thought of standing here for the rest of the night. Just being wet through and cold was enough to cope with. The windows and doors shuddered more violently than ever. Every time the door of the ladies' crashed open, we jumped out of our skin. It was always unpredictable. We were exhausted.

Pete got up, so I went to sit down on the toilet for a while. But I found I didn't like it after all. We decided to walk about a bit. Both the boys had had the sense to bring their torches. Even so it felt very spooky.

We crept down the passage, passing the ghostly toilets on the left with the even darker black holes of the showers on the right. At the bottom we turned left. There were a few more shower cubicles at the bottom end, and further along, an ironing board standing in a small alcove. Half the alcove floor was flooded.

We turned left again, tentatively following the torchlight, and realised we were now in the ladies' area. At the very moment we were passing the outer door, it burst open and slammed against the outside wall like a great explosion, letting in the wind and rain with an almighty gust. We leapt in the air, gasping with fright.

When our hearts had stopped thumping and we'd composed ourselves again, we continued up the ladies' side, where the toilets backed onto the men's in a mirror-image layout. We arrived at the wash area to find it very dimly lit and the floor flooded. We might as well go back to where we'd been before.

The boys shone their torches all around as we skulked back, half expecting someone to jump out on us at any moment, such was the nervous state we were in.

Above the ironing alcove, their torchlight picked up a black shape. They directed the beams upwards. We could see an opening to a loft with a ladder across it. Malc and I steadied the ironing board, while Pete climbed onto it to reach the ladder. He struggled to undo the catch, then we helped him lower it to the ground. Cautiously we climbed up to investigate. We were desperate to find somewhere to lie down, but also fearful of the storm that was ranting and raging just the other side of this corrugated tin roof.

The torchlight revealed a loft full of junk - old tents, new dustbins, sacks, swings, slides, dinghies and everything else to do with a seaside campsite. At the far end was what looked like a large flat sofa or a short fat bed-base. It was piled high with broken bits of hardboard, with an old canvas tent or sail thrown over. Maybe we could lie on top of it all and get some rest.

Downstairs, the dog kept barking. It had become more of a nuisance than a diversion and we were glad to get away from it. Pete and Malc took a spare sack down and laid it on the dry side of the floor in the ironing alcove. Maybe he would lie down eventually.

We made our way back to the sofa bed and with immense

relief, tinged with trepidation, climbed aboard. We turned and fidgeted for ages, trying to get rid of lumps and creases in the wrong places. Finally we were as comfy as we could hope to be, curled up with our knees sticking into each other, comforted by our closeness.

The storm was wicked. In the blackness of the attic our imaginations were running riot. What with the noise from outside and the continuous barking of the dog within, we didn't get much respite at all. Even so, Pete set his alarm for 6 am, so that we could be out of this loft before the proprietresse found us trespassing here. I couldn't have cared less, but it worried the boys. It only gave us an hour and a bit, anyway.

The blasted dog wouldn't stop. When the side door was next flung open he went outside. But the door slammed shut on him and he was unable to get back in. Out in the tempest he barked even more. We thought he was barking mad!

We couldn't get to sleep. Our legs were freezing. Pete got up to look for something to cover us with and came back with a bit of old sisal matting. It was prickly and probably filthy but it stopped the flow of air on our wet trousers. We dozed intermittently and Pete's alarm didn't go off, after all. He must have changed his mind once we'd got comfy and switched it off. Anyway, who, in their right minds would come to clean the toilets in THIS?

It was past seven o'clock when we reluctantly made our way down the ladder. We didn't know what we were going to do next. There was no sign of the dog.

The wind had lost some of its ferocity now and the rain

was more intermittent. As it was beginning to get light, Pete and Malc were very keen to see what state their tents were in. They ran down the drive, found the tents all flattened and ran straight back, wet through once again.

Our next decision was to go out for short intervals, retrieve as much as we could carry and bring it back up to the toilet block. We dashed down to our plot and pulled up the remaining pegs around Pete's inner tent, heaved it up complete with all its contents and struggled back to the toilets. It was a memorable moment. As the boys dropped the dead weight onto the floor, the water gushed out all over so that we had to jump in the air.

We extricated our various belongings from inside it. My nylon bag of clothes, which had been part of Pete's luxury bed, might as well have been dropped into the sea, it was so sodden. I found our Brittany Ferries brochure inside, almost falling to bits, and opened it carefully. I needed to find the ferry times for the next few days before it disintegrated, jotting them down in my diary (which luckily I kept in a plastic bag). We began stacking everything around the edges of the washroom floor.

When the next lull came, we ran out again to see what we could rescue. In the middle section we found our pans, bowls, kettle and various beakers and containers, all safe and sound. The rest of our wine, lemonade and milk were still there in their bottles. Miraculously, our five eggs were lying on the wet grass, but the egg box had completely disintegrated!

Malc took as much as he could carry and dashed back up

to the toilet block. Pete and I stayed on to grab a few extra bits. Suddenly, an absolute wall of rain struck us, knocking us sideways, leaving us grovelling on the grass and gasping for breath. We were TOTALLY drenched. Water poured from our clothes and shoes as we struggled to stand. It was an altogether strange and frightening experience. We raced back to the toilet block. I leaned over a sink and burst into tears. I felt UTTERLY defeated.

Between my sobs I happened to notice the distraught looks on the boys' faces. I realised how much they were depending on me and felt truly ashamed. I mustn't let *them* down. We were all in this together. So I forced myself to stop the self-pity and got on with the job in hand.

We went back for more belongings, but left the remains of Malc's tent where it was. There was just no more space in the washroom. I went through my bag of clothes, wringing everything out and lining the backs of the sinks with them. I kept wondering how on earth we were going to ride our bikes with all this extra weight to carry, but soon realised that we wouldn't be going anywhere.

The storm began to subside. A young man came rushing into the washroom, but he stepped back in amazement as he saw all the flotsam on the floor and looked embarrassed. Then an elderly man came in with a towel round his neck. He didn't know what to make of it all. With his bald head and very round face, we recognised him as the fisherman to whom we'd spoken yesterday. He ummed and ahed and spoke to Pete, because I wasn't really in a state to listen. After a while he suggested that we ought to take everything to the games room. Then he realised that we couldn't. They closed it at the end of August. Today was September 1st.

He washed a bit and shaved a bit, in a ponderous fashion, trying to come up with some solution. Then he said we could *ask* for the games room to be opened. He finished his shaving and left. We carried on with our wringing-out tasks.

A little later the fisherman returned to say that *he* had arranged for the games room to be reopened. We thanked him warmly, feeling slightly uplifted.

Looking outside, we saw patches of blue sky getting closer and the rain beginning to peter out. We grabbed armfuls of our possessions and struggled down to the games room. As we arrived, the proprietress was just opening the back doors for us. They resembled large sliding garage doors like the ones on the new toilet block, but they rattled so much in the wind that she had to pull them shut again. She opened up a side door instead. We now realised that she was also the farmer's wife from the top of the site.

We dropped the first loads onto the floor. I looked around to plan what I was going to do with everything. A salamander was crouching in the corner behind the door. We'd never seen one before and the boys wouldn't touch it, so I picked it up cautiously, hoping it wouldn't bite me, and placed it on the rockery outside.

Backwards and forwards we went until everything but the tents was in there. I laid clothes all over the three table-tennis tables and also on the wooden tables and benches in the TV room. I draped Malc's inner tent onto a broom hedge behind the rockery, fastening the loops onto various twigs. But it was the wind that held it in place.

The sun was now beautiful. Pete erected his inner tent to dry out. We'd found the flysheets. They'd blown over the hedges and were several plots up the site. We'd even discovered our little box of raisins up near the farm. It still had three raisins left inside. We shared them!

As I emerged from the toilets with our last few possessions, Pete came to tell me that we'd been invited to breakfast by a couple whose caravan was near the games room. Malc was already there. Pete had sent him on ahead so that he'd be forced to make conversation without our help.

Underneath a large awning, which was attached to the caravan, we joined Malc at a table. This caravan belonged to friends of our fisherman and his wife. All four of them were sitting inside the van, talking to us through the open door. The two ladies came out with a big pot of coffee and kept inviting us to tuck into the food on the table. Again and again they brought more coffee and urged us to keep eating. They were super. If I hadn't been sitting in wet pants, trousers and shoes, this would have been bliss – just bread, butter and Camembert cheese, but it seemed like a feast. I'd also never realised how nice black chicory coffee could taste. As for conversation, all I could say was "merci" repeatedly. Nothing else would come to mind. We spent ages eating and drinking, and afterwards, felt ready to face the day.

The first thing I did was to find our other three pairs of

shoes and prop them up on the rockery in the sun. I removed all the insoles and wove them amongst the rockery plants to stop them from blowing away. Then I put the camping mats outside and pinned them down at one end with spare rockery stones. They flapped about merrily. We hadn't told a soul about the loft. We'd even put the ladder back, with great difficulty.

The farmer's wife asked me if I'd like to borrow a jogging suit and T-shirt. I didn't really want to, as I intended getting my other trousers dry before long. Besides, I didn't want to have a better deal than the boys. They also had wet trousers, socks and shoes, although their anoraks did cover their bottoms better than mine did. Anyway I couldn't make her understand, and I didn't want to seem ungrateful. So when she came back a bit later with a lovely blue outfit, I accepted graciously. But by then I'd found the dryer. It was in a shed next to the new toilet block and I was in the process of drying my first batch of clothes. The dryer was an old rattley thing, which ran on gas. I'd discovered this when I'd looked behind and seen fierce flames shooting up from inside.

I might have spent a fortune drying clothes but soon realised how quickly my 2-franc pieces were being swallowed up. I'd have to sort out some clotheslines. I returned to the games room with the collie now tagging on behind. I found every bit of string we possessed and put up two lines, stretching from the swings to a strong bush behind the rockery. As I could only find eight pegs, anything that could be was threaded onto the line. To do this, of course, I had to keep undoing one end. As I threaded on the T-shirts one by one, like beads on a necklace, it became heavier and heavier and was soon extremely hard to tie back onto the swing support.

Malc's and my sleeping bags were the wettest. I climbed onto a swing, wobbling dangerously, and threw them over the top bar. You couldn't get a stronger line than that, but they were in danger of taking flight, so I borrowed four strong pegs I'd seen on a nearby clothesline and secured them with those.

During my treks up and down the site I'd seen lots of destruction. One caravan had had its corner split open from top to bottom, exposing the interior. Loads of awnings were ripped to shreds or hanging off. Because the season was coming to an end, not many caravans had been occupied the previous night.

That morning, the campsite became a hive of activity. Groups of people arrived to do repairs or tow their caravans away. The man to whom the pegs must have belonged arrived to fetch his caravan. I handed him the pegs without any explanation, hoping he'd see my problem.

I don't know what Malc and Pete did with their morning but I didn't seem to be getting much help. Our collie had taken an interest in a dog on the other side of the hedge; it was Chloe.

As the sun came round I decided to pull the sliding doors right back so that I could lay the sleeping bags on the sunniest table, nearest the door. I'd found it difficult to keep them on the swings anyway. Now I had to make sure they wouldn't fall onto the floor, as there were still huge puddles inside. I arranged wet clothes all over the other two tables. It was a perfect drying day.

In the afternoon, Pete came down to say that he'd put his tent up in a different place, behind a good hedge. He wanted Malc to try to mend his tent and put that up as well. I went back with Pete and we collected all Malc's tent bits. We saw Malc playing with the collie and called him over. He said he didn't want to sleep in the tent any more, he'd sooner sleep in the loft. But we managed to change his mind.

Our first task was to straighten the three sections of the broken pole. We then had to find a way of connecting them together again. The connecting pieces had snapped off.

Pete found a piece of stick and cut off two short lengths to fit inside the pole tubing. I wrapped sticking plaster around these to make a tight fit, then we rammed the sections together. We used more sticking plaster round the outside to hold everything in place. The result was a rather bent pole, but it seemed strong enough.

Malc put up his tent. He'd come round to the idea of sleeping in it again, now it was mended. He didn't mind that it was rather saggy as he'd be able to sleep in the middle tonight. I'd be in Pete's tent.

I got out my sewing kit and made a few more repairs to Malc's tent. Pete spent ages titivating his, making sure the sides were absolutely taut so that there would be plenty of room for the two of us.

The collie went to sleep for a while, in the narrow gap between the tents and the hedge. I wished I could find out to whom he belonged. I didn't really want to be responsible for him and I certainly couldn't afford to feed him.

Now that everything was in hand I went up to the shop. It was teatime already and we hadn't had a bite to eat since that French breakfast. The shop had no bread at all, which was a great shame because it was cheap, it filled us up and we liked it. I bought a large tin of ravioli, three pears and not much else.

Next I took the borrowed clothes back to the farmer's wife in the camp office and thanked her very much. When I told her that I hadn't yet paid for last night, I couldn't understand her reply. (She had a habit of gabbling on, even after I'd told her that I didn't understand). However, I could pick up something about us standing in the toilets all night, so I assumed she wasn't going to charge us.

There was no bread for sale in the camp shop either. How was I going to fill up my boys? The farmer's wife said they might have some up at the shop, but I told her I'd already been there and they hadn't. She then offered me one of her own loaves but I'd have to wait until after closing time for it. She was being so kind to me.

Outside the camp shop, another dog was pestering our collie. It was similar in size and colour and persisted in following us back up to the tents. I kept turning round to shoo it away; it was enough trouble having just one dog tagging onto us. But it wouldn't give up. In the end, I had to chase them both away. They were cavorting around in a very improper manner and we were trying to eat our ravioli.

The farmer's wife drove down to bring us a baguette and refused to take any money for it. I was immensely grateful, although, if I could have done, I'd have had two loaves from her and paid for both. She went back to the car, then called Pete over. He was the only one she could really converse with. They drove off leaving me wondering what on earth was going on.

Pete returned ten minutes later, looking smug and dangling a key from his finger. We had been offered the use of a caravan that night (in an emergency, if our tents "departed").

When she had gone, we toyed with the idea of sleeping in the caravan anyway. The trouble was, now that we'd expended so much time in mending the tents, we were really looking forward to spending the night in them. Pete in particular had spent most of the day making everything just right. He'd pegged up the back of the ground sheet in the middle tent to stop any draughts. Then he'd attached elastic bungees (the ones we used for keeping the rolls on our bikes) from various points inside the tent, each with a specific purpose to hold something in place. It all seemed quite cosy.

However, it was still extremely windy. If more rain were to come in the night, the wind might increase with it. We really needed a good night's sleep. Tomorrow, we had at least 50 miles to cycle. Therefore, with slight reluctance, we chose the caravan and went down to have a look at it.

It was rather old and squat but quite a novelty. There was a double bed that let down from the wall, which Pete bagged first. He said that as he'd got us the caravan, he was having first choice. Malc argued with him because, as it was his turn to have a tent to himself, in theory it was his turn to have a double bed for the night.

Pete, being Pete and being a Leo, won the argument, so Malc and I would have to make do with the two narrow bunk beds which were either side of the table at the other end. I told Malc there'd be loads of room once we'd taken the table down. I walked over to it purposefully. It was made of thick chipboard and folded in two. As I was pulling it about to see how it was fixed, it suddenly went THUD, endways onto my big toe. I howled.

I sat on the bunk and cried and cried. It was *so* painful. The boys sat on the opposite bunk and laughed and laughed. Pete *did* show a bit of concern when I kept on and on. He leaned over and said "Aaah!", putting a hand on my shoulder and grinning from ear to ear. After a while though I thought to myself what a big baby I was being. Pete had put up with his swollen toe all the holiday and had hardly made any fuss. So – now we both had a sore big toe on the right foot. Life must go on.

We went over to the beach to fill in time before dark, with me limping along behind the boys, not wanting to join in their fun. But by now, we were quite excited about the prospect of sleeping in the caravan and in the end we couldn't wait until darkness fell. Soon we were snug in our bunks.

* * * * *

I was the first to wake and find myself in strange surroundings. I'd slept like a log, although I could remember hearing heavy rain during the night. It was very stuffy in the caravan and my mouth tasted like a sewer.

I tried to look out of the window, which was running with condensation. So was the window at the end of the bunk where the water had overflowed the ledge and was running down the wall towards my feet. I pulled them up away from it and lay down again, impatiently waiting for the boys to wake up. I couldn't help making comparisons with sleeping in a tent, where it never got stuffy. I just wanted to let in some air.

Pete and Malc awoke simultaneously. I immediately jumped out of bed and tried to open a window, but they were all rusted up. The boys were really annoyed. They weren't properly awake yet. In desperation I opened the top half of the door. Pete complained about the draught, so I closed it again. I decided to get dressed straight away. I needed fresh air.

My toe was now extremely sore. I'd expected to have a wonderfully black toenail to prove how much it had hurt but alas, all that showed was a fine purple line – me, with a reputation for bruising like a banana!

I thought we ought to be out of the caravan before the farmer's wife came down to the office. However, the boys had no intention of rushing. They were savouring the luxury of lying in a bed.

Eventually, we locked the caravan and took our sleeping bags back to the tents, with me hobbling behind. (If I'd been brave enough, I'd have put a hole through the toenail to let the pressure out).

The tents were beautifully dry inside; no wet edges anywhere. It seemed such a shame that after spending so much time improving them, we'd not used them. Never mind, we'd all had a jolly good night's sleep.

I felt guilty that we were leaving the caravan unaired and full of condensation. I'd have to tell the farmer's wife that we'd slept in there, so that she could air it out. Perhaps she'd think we'd taken advantage of her kindness. After all, the caravan had been offered as a last resort.

I found her cleaning sinks in the washrooms. Returning the key, I made a big issue of how well we'd slept in her caravan. At least she'd know we were extremely grateful. She was very gracious.

By now our tummies were rumbling, but the pantry was empty. I counted all the money I had left and found one F100 note, F30 of my own spending money (with which I'd planned to buy presents) and a handful of small change. That was it, apart from an amount I'd put by for our camping costs. I gave Pete the note, as he'd offered to go up to the shop for cereals. We knew they had only one variety left on the shelves, called Choco Pops.

Pete suggested that Malc should take our water bottles up to the farm to be filled with milk. I gave Malc the small change, but he was worried in case it wasn't enough. He didn't know how much milk the bottles would hold. "One and a half litres," Pete told him, irritably. But Malc was still anxious that he wouldn't know what to say if he didn't have enough money. Impatient with Malc's dithering, Pete went with him. It was on the way to the shop anyway.

Malc was tickled pink that the farmer had filled our little bottles straight from a milk tanker which just happened to be parked in the farmyard. What's more, he'd refused to take any money. The Choco Pops however were almost F20. We hoped we'd like them.

We didn't. They were mushy and tasted synthetic, but we had two bowlfuls each anyway and finished the box.

Now to get packed up. The annoying thing was, we couldn't take Malc's tent pole apart. It was stuck solid. (Of course it was all Mum's fault, using all that sticking plaster). None of us could separate the three sections. We pulled and pulled, but nothing budged. In desperation I gripped the end of the pole with my teeth while Pete yanked hard on the other end. Bingo. It came apart. My teeth had proved to be the strongest tool of all.

Everyone on the site was very chatty today and went out of their way to talk to us. Our nearest neighbour asked us where we'd spent the night. We'd obviously been missed.

I went to the office to pay our dues and bought a lovely baguette which had just been delivered. Then I amalgamated my remaining food and camping money. In all, I had F124.5 (£12.45) to get us home. That was apart from the F30 I was hanging on to as a last resort. I doubted the boys had any of their own spending money left. What I did know, however, was that all our toilet paper had gone and we'd been saving paper bags as a substitute.

We went down to say farewell and thank you to the fishermen and their wives, who in turn gave us their best wishes. Then without more ado we pushed our loaded bikes up to the farm to thank the farmer and his wife for all their help. Now it was time to set off on the last leg of our holiday. Holiday? It didn't feel like one any more, even if we were wearing shorts.

Since last year, when we'd discovered the easier route through St. Nic (via the Roman road), there was no way we'd opt for the hilly coastal road with our loaded bikes. So we left Pentrez Plage through the back gate at the top of the site. We weren't feeling sad; we weren't really feeling anything at all as we turned round for one last look at the bay. The big storm had numbed our emotions somewhat.

Barely five miles beyond St. Nic, it began to pour with rain. We were already wearing anoraks, but Malc wanted to put his trousers on. Pete and I wouldn't stop for him, not wishing to dally, with all the miles of cycling ahead of us.

Near the village of Argol we were passed by a wedding party – several beribboned cars overtook us, hooting their horns madly. Less than a mile further on another wedding party passed by. This group included a coach full of frantically-waving guests in all their finery. We waved back, feeling a little more cheery, especially now that the rain had stopped.

Soon we were on the main road leading to the Pont de Térénez. After descending the steep hill alongside the Forêt de Landévennec, we negotiated the left-hand bend onto the bridge and just kept going. Last year we'd been over-awed with the wonderful scenery here. Now we seemed blasé. Maybe the steep climb on the other side of the bridge was dominating our thoughts.

But the ascent was less arduous than we'd feared. We just kept the pedals turning at a slow steady pace, barely glancing at the beautiful estuary of the river Aulne below us.

Near Le Faou we spotted loads of gorgeous blackberries growing up a wall. We stopped abruptly and began greedily cramming them into our mouths. Realising how hungry we were, we searched for a shop.

The outskirts had altered quite a lot since last year, spoiling the look of this quaint little town. New roads had been constructed and also a brand new supermarket. In it I purchased the cheapest of crisps, biscuits and bananas that I could find. We ate these sitting low down on the steeply-sloping bank surrounding its new car park, to shelter from the wind. The grass on the bank was just beginning to grow, but there were stark thistles sprouting out everywhere.

We followed the signs out of town heading for Sizun. I didn't recognise the road from last year, but Pete and Malc could remember it.

Minutes up the road we heard a loud hiss. Damn! Malc's tyre had punctured. We could do without punctures, especially one in the back wheel where the luggage had to be removed. But we all mucked in to speed things up, even though my only input was to take a new tube out of its box and afterwards, provide a wetted rag for the boys to wipe their grimy hands on. The nice thing was, Pete and Malc were working as a team.

Only a couple of miles further on, *my* tyre punctured. Sod's law! Luckily, it was in the front wheel this time. We'd gone all holiday without any punctures. Now we'd had two in less than half an hour. But the boys jumped in to do the honours and again I didn't get my hands dirty. This time the inner tube needed a patch sticking on. We didn't have another spare tube.

Thorns proved to be the cause of both punctures – presumably from the blackberry bushes. We continued cycling, hoping that no more of them were insidiously working their way into our tyres.

Suddenly, Pete's bike swerved off course as his tent roll lurched sideways, falling onto the mudguard. NO! Not the blasted pannier rack again!

Pete jumped off his bike, unhooked his roll and panniers and flung them onto the ground in exasperation. I tried to keep my cool by looking for the (ever diminishing) roll of plaster for him to make his usual repair. As I unrolled it, Malc cut it into lengths with my little scissors.

Meanwhile, hearing our commotion, a herd of curious cows lumbered up to watch. They stared vacantly over the hedge; a long row of ruminating black and white faces. We couldn't help but laugh.

Pete found it harder to take the old sticking plaster *off* the spanner and screwdriver (which was holding the rack in place), than to actually mend it. But by using loads more plaster he made quite a good bodge. We still had about 25 more miles to cycle to reach Roscoff. Hopefully the rack would last that long.

Skirting the western edge of the Monts D'Arrée – the high

hills in the middle of Finistère - we reflected that bad luck always comes in threes. Well, we'd done our penance now. Soon we'd be in Sizun, which was past the halfway mark.

But our troubles were not yet over. For when Malc's bike jolted over a bump, there was an ominous CRACK. *His* pannier rack had broken. BLAST and DAMNATION! Now what? We didn't have another spare screwdriver or spanner to stick over this break. What's more, we hardly had any plaster left.
How the hell were we going to mend it? We dilly-dallied. We weren't panicking, just *extremely* annoyed. Somehow we would have to tie it with string.

Good old Pete. He got out his penknife and cut a thick stick from the hedgerow while I found the string in my handlebar bag. Most of it was cord-like, thick enough for clotheslines, but there was also a small roll of the thin stuff – more cotton-like. It didn't seem strong enough, but that was all we had.

But this idea of Pete's didn't seem to work. The rack support was a flat section of metal and the round stick wouldn't stay in place. If only we'd had a flat piece of wood.

Then Malc remembered the six-inch wooden ruler he had in his bag. Goodness knows why he'd brought it on holiday – a sort of mascot, I suppose. Reluctantly, he gave it to Pete. But it was too wide. It would have to be made narrower. It was a lovely old, varnished hardwood ruler. Malc treasured it and was visibly dismayed to see Pete butchering it with his penknife.

I suggested smearing the under side of the ruler with our puncture-repair glue, to stop it slipping while we bound the string round it. It certainly helped. But there was no way this bit of ruler was going to support the weight of Malc's tent roll and panniers. Somehow we had to attach a cross-member to both the bike frame and the upright.

Pete came up with an idea. He would use his bit of stick, angled from the forks up to the rack to form a triangle. It wasn't long enough. He searched the hedgerow for ages, looking for a strong enough, long enough piece. I was getting really anxious about the time. Would we reach our destination before dark?

Malc wasn't just standing around. *He'd* had a good idea as well. He was unravelling a length of cord into three separate pieces, thin enough to bind the stick onto the frame.

Using the remaining plaster and the three lengths of cord, we finally completed our clumsy repair. And just as an extra precaution we smeared rubber-glue solution over all the string and cord. Bumps and potholes must now be avoided at all costs.

At a garage in Sizun we refilled our water bottles and shared the crusty baguette which I had hoped to keep for supper. But we really needed a treat after all these setbacks.

Soon we were cycling towards Landivisiau, with its confusing ring road. But once we'd negotiated that, we reached the main road towards St. Pol-de-Léon and sailed along, grateful for the smoothness of the tarmac.

We missed the turning for the supermarket, so we carried on towards town, taking the next turning instead. Rushing to get there before the 8 pm closing time, we somehow got split up. Malc and I rounded the corner to find that Pete had vanished without trace. Which street had he taken? My first reaction was panic, for we had no means of communication. But this subsided when I surmised that, one way or another, we'd either meet up at the supermarket or at the Roscoff campsite – God willing!

Malc and I found the supermarket in the nick of time. One of the employees was just reaching up to bolt the doors as we raced up to them. He turned to the woman on the checkout. She looked at her watch, then smiled at us and nodded. He let us in. We were so glad, because apart from our Famous Five eggs (which had survived the storm) we had nothing else to eat.

I dashed round the shelves and grabbed a baguette, plus a pack of chocolate bars and a bottle of cider for our final treat. Just in time, I remembered to buy more plasters for Pete's toe. After paying for these, I barely had enough money left for camping. However, seeing Pete waiting outside made up for all my worries.

As we rode towards our old campsite, I remembered that I still owed for two nights' camping from last time. I wasn't even sure I had enough money for tonight. We'd have to find an alternative.

It was dusk when we reached the entrance gates. We continued past them towards Roscoff, looking for the little lane that led down to our tailboard bay.

There *was* a lane beyond the perimeter of the campsite but we weren't sure if it was the one we wanted. We took it anyway, pushing the bikes carefully, for fear of breaking our repairs.

Seeing a group of large sand dunes, we made a quick decision to erect the tents amongst them, if there was enough space. There was no time to hang about; darkness was encroaching fast.

We were worried that Malc's tent pole might not slot together very well after all that tugging to pull it apart, and just hoped it would do its job. If the sides sagged a bit, it wouldn't really matter, because it was still Malc's turn to have a tent to himself. I wondered how he felt about sleeping alone in this rather remote spot, especially as we wouldn't be able to join up the tents this time.

With the tents pitched rather haphazardly but sheltered from the wind, I got out the stove to do the cooking while Pete shone his torch onto my little frying pan. I couldn't be bothered to beat the five eggs together and then separate them into three equal amounts for omelettes, so I fried two eggs each for the boys and had one myself. The baguette was gorgeous and I made sure I had my fair share of that.

I set the kettle on the stove for Pete's toe-soaking water, then we sat in his tent eating the chocolate and sipping the cider. This was our final treat of the holiday, although I think we'd rather have crawled straight into bed, we were so tired. Like last year, we'd have to get up really early to be at the ferry terminal by 7 am for the 8 am sailing. But at least this year we had plenty of torch power to see what we were doing.

Homecoming

Roscoff to Stroud

Soon after midnight we were awoken by the sound of a car creeping down the lane. It stopped only yards from our tents and the engine was turned off. Pete and I lay still, breathing quietly but all ears, rigid with apprehension. We hoped the tents were well hidden by the dunes. It would terrify us if someone saw them and came snooping round in the black of night. We hadn't a clue if Malc was awake. I thought he might be scared stiff, all alone in his tent.

Several nerve-racking minutes passed in silence. Then two doors opened and shut quietly and a man and a woman whispered to each other in a terse manner. We listened as the sound of their footsteps faded towards the beach. Surely they weren't going for a midnight dip?

After another long silence, we heard them coming back, puffing up the slope as if they were carrying something. The boot clicked open then shut again. It sounded very suspicious. They set off for the beach again and returned once more, out of breath.

By now, we were convinced that they were smugglers, making a secret rendezvous with a boat. After their third trip they got quietly into the car and reversed slowly back up the lane. Phew! We breathed properly again. It was like being in an Enid Blyton adventure. I called softly to Malc. Yes, he *was* awake and yes, he *had* been scared. But he said he was OK now that they'd gone.

We were wide awake now, whispering excitedly to each other. Perhaps if we were to creep down to the beach we'd see a boat leaving the shore. It would most likely be a rowing boat, to negotiate the rocks. There must be a bigger vessel moored further out to sea, we thought. None of us actually wanted to get out of our warm sleeping bags to have a look, but it was fun speculating.

The wind changed soon after we'd quietened down and instead of being sheltered we were now buffeted. But even with the tents flapping we went back to sleep eventually.

Pete's alarm went off. Oh no! Was it 5.30 already? Did we have to get up? But there was no choice. We either caught the 8 am ferry or stayed in Brittany and starved to death.

With the help of the boys' front lights we decamped without too much hassle. We'd used every single tent peg to hold the tents down in these sandy dunes and it was easy enough to locate them all. The happenings in the night were still fresh on our minds and had it been daylight, we'd have been tempted to go searching for clues on the beach. "There might still be a boat hiding behind the rocks," said Malc. Anyway, it would have to remain a mystery and memory for always. Just thinking about it, though, took our minds off the tasks in hand and we managed to reach the ferry terminal by 7am.

The previous year I'd booked our return trip the day before we travelled, to make sure there would be room on board. But it really didn't seem necessary at this end of the season and everything was above board now, with Pete having an adult ticket.

While we waited to board the ferry we spoke to a Scottish couple with a tandem. They had cut short their holiday because of the bad weather and had arrived in Roscoff late the previous night, too late to find B&B accommodation. So they'd spent all night in the terminal foyer and were feeling tired out and fed up. We all had our crosses to bear and our tales to tell but right then, we didn't exactly want to talk about ours. We just let them grumble on about theirs.

The ferry due in from Cork was an hour late arriving. That didn't bode well. Were we in for another rough crossing? We waited to board our ferry with our hoods pulled up against the keen wind. Earlier, I'd seen the dreadful state of my hair in a mirror in the ladies' toilets. It was really greasy, sticking to my head. I would have to keep my hood up for the entire journey. How stupid would that look?

When we had boarded and the passengers were established in their seats, I made a recce of the ship. In a quiet corner well below deck, I found some toilets which nobody seemed to be using. I swiftly filled a sink with hot water, threw my anorak on the floor and, as speedily as possible, washed my hair with the hand soap. Rinsing it seemed to take forever, just because I wanted to be quick. I patted my hair with paper towels then stuck my head under the hand drier several times. Nobody came in. That was good. I mopped up and left everything as dry as I'd found it.

Feeling much better about myself, even though my hair looked a bit wild, I went back to join the boys. They'd begun to worry about me.

Our journey wasn't rough, as we'd expected. Even Malc was managing ok. Down in the café we bought a baguette which turned out to be really stale. Pete spied some unused butter packs and an unopened marmalade sachet abandoned on a table. As we walked past he slipped them onto our tray. They moistened the bread a bit. Then he produced some change from his pocket; just enough to buy us all a coffee.

I thought to myself how lucky I was to have these two lovely boys whom I'd enticed abroad because I was desperate for adventure but too scared to go alone. I felt so proud of them for all they'd coped with on this trip. It couldn't really be classed as a holiday; more like doing a Duke of Edinburgh's award. The really nice thing was that since the storm, they'd been much more brotherly towards each other.

We finally arrived in Plymouth without incident and were at the railway station by 2.30 pm. I hadn't found the missing rail ticket and it was far from straightforward to buy another one for just £1, as part of my family rail card deal. But eventually I managed to convince the ticket man.

I phoned Jim to tell him the time we expected to arrive in Cheltenham. Hopefully he'd meet us so that we could transfer our loads into the car. That would make the rest of our journey less arduous.

At Bristol we had only seven minutes to change platforms. In the rush, Pete's light got broken on the metal barrier of the goods van. Cycling home would be a bit tricky now. We'd have to ride close together with Pete in the middle, minus his front light.

Jim was waiting outside Cheltenham station in our old car. Although he seemed fairly pleased to see us, he didn't show much enthusiasm. We might just as well have been returning from a day's shopping trip. He asked us nothing at all about our holiday. However, he insisted on me travelling back with him in the car. I could hardly refuse, since he'd come all the way to meet us. But it wasn't what I'd planned at all.

It was decided that Pete should ride home on my bike, which still had its dynamo lights. So Jim and I put Pete's bike into the back of the car while Pete raised my bike seat to accommodate his long legs.

My eyes followed the boys wistfully as they rode off and disappeared into the dimness of the lamplight. As we overtook them I waved pathetically, feeling like a traitor, tears in my eyes. I should be sharing this last challenge of the trip with them, not riding home in a car.

What was wrong with me? I ought to have been grateful for this lift. Could I, at this end of the day, have managed the sixteen miles of cycling, all the way up the Cotswold edge in the dark, then down the other side through Painswick to Stroud, plus the final climb up Butterrow Hill to reach home? Probably not.

This holiday, unlike the previous year's when we'd had so much fun and sunshine, had clearly taught me that the grass really *isn't* greener on the other side, or the weather any better. And as we reached home, it dawned on me what I was really craving; *freedom*. This life continuously trapped on the breadline was not what I wanted, not forever. I decided that before too long, things would have to be different.

Meanwhile I hovered anxiously behind the front door, waiting for the safe return of the boys who had proved such wonderful companions on my adventures across the Channel.

Postscript

After our return in 1988, I wrote to Michael Fish, the weather man, and asked what the forecast had been on the night of that dreadful storm. He kindly sent me printouts of the appropriate weather charts and informed me that it had been just an ordinary depression. That was not what I would have called it. A friend who'd been camping with her family in Devon that same night had suffered a similar disaster. They'd had to huddle in their car all night. So it wasn't even a localised phenomenon.

These Brittany holidays marked the beginning of the end of my marriage. A few years later, after my divorce, I began working at Stroud Museum, where I remained until my retirement. However I never did manage to rise far above the breadline in spite of my best efforts, and I still hover there in my retirement!

I had one more camping holiday with both boys (around the coast of Wales) before they felt they wanted to do their own thing. I couldn't believe what a short span it had been between them becoming capable of doing it and feeling too old to come with me. I almost felt cheated. (Malc and I did go to Normandy some years later, when he was a student).

Meanwhile I joined the Stroud Cyclists Touring Club and enjoyed many trips abroad with them, several to my beloved Brittany but mostly youth hostelling, and never in tents. But nothing has ever matched the excitement and uncertainty of those first two holidays in Brittany.

As for my boys, Pete transferred his special bike parts to a lovely blue racing frame and enjoyed several spins with the Cheltenham Racing Club, until his bike was stolen from outside Stroud swimming pool the following summer. Malc joined the local athletics club and did well in many events, including throwing the discus for the South West when he was 17, competing against Geoff Capes' son.

Both boys have done really well in life. Pete went into engineering and has carved a niche for himself with a well-known oil company with his 'Fuel Save' initiatives. Malc took the artistic line, and studied illustration. He now works for a cutting-edge, award-winning firm near Bath, writing the code for games and applications for some of the most popular children's entertainment companies. They are both happily married and I hope they long remain so.